# OF SKIN AND BONES
## ~ LIFE IN VERSE ~

Mary Mansour Durel

ISBN: 978-1489531124

To my remarkable parents, Alexander Elias Mansour and Frances Muriel Wills Mansour

To my charismatic, supportive siblings, June, A.E., Esther, Scott, Edith, and Miriam

To my indomitable, courageous children, Steve, Laurie, Mike, and Melissa

Acknowledgments

To Gay W. Holland for formatting, for critiquing, for moral support, for friendship

To Ginney Etherton for publishing intricacies, for selflessness, for moral support, for friendship

To my lovely daughter Melissa Durel for formatting and editing this book and for constant moral support

To the Bandon Writers Guild and the Bandon Writers for forbearance, understanding, thoughtful appraisals, and friendship

# ROOTS

## WARMTH IN A DARK PLACE

Dark came early
and stayed late;
losses magnified guilt,
etching their numbing pattern
on the brain's cold tomb.
It was a winter solstice
all year long.

But yesterdays crept in
on a single shaft of afternoon:
Summers of sun and shadows laced with sun
and slow sun settings tangled in the sycamore by the river;
days when the valley, swollen with heat,
charged with lightning, turned
navy
purple
black
and the thunder boomed,
exploding the stagnant air.
Rain strands, right-angled,
swept the earth,
brushing up the pink scent of petunias,
settling a silver silence on the listening hills;
and the warm dark sifted in
lighting the yellow lanterns
of a thousand fireflies.

*July 9-26, 1995*


## MORE THAN MEMORY

I'd like to go out
on that softened street
with its patina of old rain,
walking barefoot,
body free as rippling water,
to inhale the brown scent of stilled dust,
wince under the peppering of a burst cloud,
and slip ecstatic into the horizon of sun.

*Dec. 23-28, 2003*

## THE SUN'S CHILDREN

"What are those?"
the little girl asked.

"Sunbeams," her mother said.
So, for years she thought
the tiny bouncing specks of dust
were children of the sun.

You have to ask the question wrong
to get the right one answered
or the dust will dance in fancy on rays that don't exist.

*June 27, 1999*


## RUNNING FREE

She always ran—
to school,
home for lunch and back,
and when she thought
she wasn't wanted
by the slow-moving girls
who walked in groups.

She ran faster than all the boys,
never seeming to compete
but more for the shearing pleasure
of keeping an edge honed
clean as a blade,
to maintain a distance.

She never stopped running,
never accepted rejection,
refused the stigma of isolation,
the retaliatory action,
moving always outward
tucked like a fist in the wind.

*June 21-July 4, 1999*

DEATH IN AN OLD MAN

It is a yellowed blur,
this death in the face of the sun.
The heat slides sticky down the flesh.
Fat-bodied flies bow lazy legs across the bed sheet.

Bones V sharply in one leg; the other knees in and out
waving pain to the abyss of consciousness and back again
to merge in animal wail from the wide dry empty mouth.
Eyes open with a veil thicker than that of sleep, web-gauze of the grave.
Hair like gray knots of steel wool banks tight to the head.
A glass of milk withers around a bent straw, blank-faced
as a child in concentration.
The buckled flyswatter melts against the wall like a used puppet.
The sharp rise of the rib cage yet speaks life.

It is a blueish blur that stirs its feathers to me,
this death in the face of the night.
The hills lie like a sleeping woman, snubbing their breasts to the dark.
Cool curtains wipe the air to rest.

The iron bars climbing one side of the bed clank
as the bone of the arm drops over their sides.
Yellow flesh clings like wet dough to the face.
A perfect foot like a bright leech hangs to the avenue of breath.
Life sits, stark white, king over the tunnel
of ribbed dark curving down the throat.
A glass of orange juice burbling froth colors the senseless glass,
unconscious as blood that colors the anemic life tubes.
The limp sheet sags like a straw doll.
The sharp fall of the rib cage yet speaks life.

*1959, Seattle*

## SLOW LEARNER

"Let's play house," the bigger girl said,
drawing a square on the ground.
"I'm the mommy, Bobby's the daddy,
and you're the baby."

"What am I supposed to do?" I asked,
watching her sweep briskly.
She froze me out.

Today I know what to do:
snuggle between pink sheets,
sense around me the whole universe
crackling with all I do not know
and offering me everything.

*Oct. 14-17, 2012*

## DEPRESSION CHILD

A penny meant
a candy bar
and sometimes
twofer.

Five would buy
an ice cream cone
and ten
a loaf of bread.

Once I found
an Indian-head.
"Save it,"
my mama said.

*Aug. 18, 2000; Jan. 7, 2001*

REMEMBERING MAMA
(Three-Cent Stamps)

I put on yesterday's dress,
high-necked round collar,
fitted waist, flared skirt;
went down yesterday's street
two blocks to the post office;
climbed up the high stairs
with yesterday's fright;
saw the woman in the cage,
and with yesterday's trembling
showed my six letters
and pushed my coins through.
She gave me eighteen stamps.
Carefully I stuck one
on each envelope
and dropped them in the slot.
The extras I took home to Mama.

In yesterday's dress,
in yesterday's house,
I wasn't made smaller
for not knowing
penny stamps were different.

*May 2- 5, 2012*

FUEL

"Mom, June's making big eyes!"
my brother would shout,
breaking the spell, the moment
a mere breath to the wind
before everything dispersed
and we were just three children
sitting on the living room rug.

Today we no longer know each other,
but the past cannot be put to bed,
tucked in, wished goodnight.
Although sluggish, the current runs
faithful as blood is faithful
a long way back, obligatory
to keep the bones warm.

*Sept. 8-14, 2008*

## ROUND GAME

Timeless in our cotton dresses,
happiness unadulterated, we spin,
the sky blue, the sun warm.

"Ring around the rosies"—
hands joined in acceptance;
"pocketful of posies"—
alert to all the possibles,
the spontaneity of the moment.

"Ashes, ashes," we chant,
unclasping hands.
"We all fall down."

*July 17-19, 2008*


## EMBERS

Sometimes on summer nights
my dad would build a fire outside
from the scraps of his carpentry.
Swirls of liquid orange light streamed upward,
a magnet for the neighbor children who came crowding,
my dad cautioning.
We brought potatoes,
my dad tucking them under with an iron poker.
Only when the fire was embers did he go inside.

The night hung softly at our backs,
humbling our voices, stretching out time.
Impatient, we retrieved with long sticks
our blackened delicacies, hard as stone,
chomping into the half-raw flesh,
scraping our teeth through an eighth inch of charcoal.

Silence moved  in. Someone stepped out the last spark
and the warm summer night reclaimed its moon and stars.
The neighbor children stumbled home through dark,
and we climbed our porch stairs into oblivion.

*Jan. 1-9, 2005*

SUMMER DARK

is fleecy, thick and humid.
If you could grasp it,
you could slice or bat it away;
but it would just keep coming,
filling all the space of the house,
moving through the walls, under the doors.

You knew the places where it lived,
where it fed, multiplying —
the attic, the unfloored basement, the linen closet;
how grudgingly it gave over to day,
withdrawing into itself.

Yet it was never truly gone:
It held more reality than the light.

*April 22-25, 2009*


WHEN MINUTES WERE LONG

She was a little girl
orphaned in outlook
but unaware of it
because it did not matter then.

"I hear cats' toenails," she said.

Her mother, puzzled,
listened for the sound,
then queried:
"Where is it coming from?"

She led the way to the bedroom wall.
They stood quiet, their heads atilt.

"Oh," her mother said,
wide-eyed as her daughter,
"It's the icicles falling off the roof."

*Sept. 23-26, 2009*

LYING IN WAIT

Nyah, nyah!
You can't catch me.

How about tomorrow?
Deep down,
the entrails curl and moil,
the usual treachery.
Arms, legs, and shoulders fret,
the stomach frenzied
over what threatens.

As ever, morning seeps in.
You dress routinely,
swallow what food you can,
and step outside.

Smack – right up the side of the head.

*April 10-15, 2007*


NIGHT RAIN

Spent and unspent the hours lie
until the sudden rain splits against the glass
and  another night from years ago revives.

> Windows must be shut against this deluge,
> but the minutes go by and the fine drops
> spitting from the sill cool the sizzle of my face and body.
> My sister, older by eighteen months,
> comes in clothed in reproach,
> closes the window and pads away.

> Breathless in the steamy heat, I sneak from bed,
> ease up the window's wooden frame
> just enough for air to swoosh in,
> knowing it is naughty,
> knowing what water does to wood,
> knowing also that soon the rain will stop,
> the sweet wet breeze flood the room,
> and I will pull up the sheet to cover my little shivers.

*Oct. 13, 2006; July 13 – 15, 2007*

RECESS

Take two giant steps.
May I?

Permission must be granted;
the rules of the game are rigid.

I wait, on tiptoe,
planted insecurely
to solid earth.

Time wavers.
The players fade.
The schoolhouse is boarded up,
the road paved over.

No one answers.

*July 15- Aug. -10, 2006*


TRANSCENDENCE

A shift of the shadows
and the chair walks
stiff-legged, footless,
scaring the dark
into grotesqueries.

The dresser shoulders in,
the curtains writhe,
the rug bristles its fur,
the closet bulges outward.

Mama!

And the shadows are gone.

*Γcb. 27- Mar-6, 2010*

## INDECIPHERABLES

Nights should be silent,
but the child I am keeps rousing.

What startled the  curtain,
tugged at the sheet,
ticked on the window,
breathed near the door?

What creeps about
when the lights are out,
everyone in bed,
the air expectant?

The shadows come,
their substance unknown,
turning and twisting,
quivering and bobbling,
contracting, expanding —
nightmares, their own.

*Aug. 5 – Sept. 10, 2005; March 12, 2006*


## COMING UP EMPTY

It wasn't called a dead-end.
There was a creek there,
the color of dried mustard.

One summer an old woman
screaming and waving her arms ran down it
straight into the water,
her son in pursuit,
his naked white feet flapping like ducks.
He wrapped her streaming body close
and took her back.

I know that feeling,
wanting to run straight into nowhere.
But how would I survive
if someone brought me back?

*May 27-29, 2005*

## THE WALLFLOWER

She sat with bone-locked knees,
free to chart the inner springs of expectation;
to taste, untried, the colors of the flesh.

Hope prickled down her arms
and quivered back to flush her face,
a mirror of her innocence.

She sat, her body fledgling,
aware of every moving male.
A pause from one, a glance her way —
could she rise, her limbs all needled?
No hand extended.
Her mouth went weak,
a twitch of shame for her mistake.

She sat, hands primly crossed, open
to the turbulence of timed response —
a sprite released
who caught the nuance of every glance
and whirled uncoupled through each dance.

*July 9-18, 1993; Sept. 6, 1994; March 13, 2005*


## WINGING IT

In dreams I flew.
Child that I was,
I knew it was true.

For years I wondered,
asking the air if loft
came only when I slept.

Yet sometimes now
when the sky burns blue,
in a wink I rise
above the earth
to cuddle with clouds
and ride their surf.

*Feb. 24-25, 2013*

11

WHEN THE WORLD WAS ROUND

I lived in a house
where one could dream
enough dreams to last a lifetime;
where the senses pricked
the mind to fashion a street
with so many turns and twists
it would never dead-end.
No turn was the same as another,
nor was there reason to turn back,
to retrace a first impression.

It was a house where no one searched
for love or acceptance
because those were just there,
sustenance in a period of grace.

*June 27-Aug. 27, 2012*


AFTER HOURS

Before you come
the tooth is under the pillow.
As always the moon will edge up slowly
a bare rim of maybe,
a lone bird chirp will spark the night,
dogs exchange bedtime yips.

When the clock has spun out its hours of darkness,
the moon faded, the sky a cacophony of birds,
the dogs tugging apart an old sock;
when the shivers of expectation have grown old,
only then will you have come and gone —
the exchange a single coin.

*Aug. 1-2, 2009*

EVOCATIONS
(Mid-1930'S)

The house —
weathered the color of old sky —
comfortably eased into the slope
running down to the creek.
On roller skates
we bumpily floundered
across the rough boards
of its wrapped-around porch,
watched by the white-faced neighbor
from her window next door.

The outhouse,
a cabin of raw wood
unfamiliar to us but replicated
near every residence,
perched in the back yard.
Reluctant to use it,
we sneaked there, covert.

The creek,
thickly sticky with ooze,
the stench of unidentifiables
rotting among tin cans and broken bottles —
the swimway for Doc Loomis' ducks—
trickled its way to the wide brown Kanawha.

"Where the green creek
meets the pink river,"
Mama would sing at sunset.
"That's where we live."

We immersed in our moments.

No photographs exist.

*Nov. 3-9, 2012*

## THE FIGURE-EIGHT

The air stiff
breaking against the breath,
the house one huge shiver,
and we racing through the dark hall,
down the stairs, into the kitchen
where warmth was held
within closed doors,
the little gas heater blazing,
the oven door open,
and my mom in a Kelly green sweater,
the newest baby tucked up in the carriage.

Outside, the river freezing
against the frozen creek
and the frozen ground,
the big boy Junior
flowing along it on ice skates
and I in my bulky brown snowsuit
enthralled, on my knees,
clearing the snow from the ice
to make him a larger pathway;
I, wanting to move like that,
fluid with the sharp wind
and execute a figure-eight
right where the creek joined the Kanawha River.
I knew I could do that if I had skates.

I saved my money a whole year
until I had the $2.98 Sears-Roebuck wanted
for the white ones like Sonja Heinie's.
I got to use them only twice,
never achieving a figure-eight,
S-ing out and back to join two rounds
to end at the very place
where I began.

*March 8-11, 1999*

## WHERE THE EYE RESTS

So it is that the shadow
commands the attention,
teasing the senses
to believe that it came first.

Out of ripe dark it sprang
subject only to light;
able to filter into bone,
sinew, and flesh;
squirm between the feet,
emerge before or behind,
giant or pygmy
depending on the position of sun,
candle, electric bulb, fire.

Once when I was sick,
my uncle made rabbits, horses, and birds
appear on the bedside wall
by flexing his fingers
in front of the lamp.

So I learned shadows could be regulated,
planned, forced into shapes
differing from the shaper,
not just in substance
but in the mind.

*May 27-30, 2004*


## FEATHERING

Especially in the full bud of June
morning tweaks memory
from its hidden cave.

The creek flows mudbrown
into the picklegreen of the Kanawha.
The boat steady,
I push off from The Point,
dipping and feathering the oars,
skimming out past the juncture—
a whisper on the water—
just beyond the reach of earth.

*July 1, 2001*

## THE MIDDLE ROOM

I've never grown up.
I'm still going down the long hall
past that room where night seeped
into the corners, the light falling away
until it was one huge pocket of dark
holding silence like a caught breath—
the middle room that we had to pass
on our way to bed.

Nothing there went bump in the night,
not my grandmother's dress dancing in the closet,
not the wheeled toy box shifting its contents,
nor even the Christmas ornaments twinkling out of season.
It was all those unknowns shaping and reshaping themselves
that silenced silence.

"Close the door if it frightens you," my mama said.

But even then I felt them soft as down,
shriveling in the air like dying balloons.

*May 6-12, 1998*


## FROZEN WOMB

In the valley in the winter
the cold is like a knife,
sharp and cruel, incisive.

Our nostrils sticking shut,
we run for warmth, puff
mist balloons of breath.
Clumsily we stumble
on the ridges of frozen earth.

Death is under those ridges
curled tight as an embryo
in a mulch of frozen grass.
We barely scratch the surface,
our feet etch the ice of earth;
but in the stillness of valley winter
one sound could trigger birth.

*Nov. 27, 1974; Dec. 25 –27, 2009*

AND

there were in the same country
Baby Jesus away in a manger,
Santa Claus away at the North Pole.

December pours in lush with rain hinting of snow.
Our old house prickles with hope,
crackles with things unseen,
sparkles with red bulbs twinned in the long windows.
Fruitcake mellows in the bread drawer.
Two blocks away Box 123 in the post office
floods with Christmas cards,
as many flowing out from here, 9 Orchard Avenue.

In the night imagination grows rosy
creating the stable, the Baby,
and the one magnificent star.
The dark is so soft I can feel it with my hand.
Under Mama's old raccoon coat I am warm.

Bells jingle, reindeer prance.
The Baby is light in his mother's arms.

*Dec. 12-19, 2008*


IN THE SOLAR PLEXUS

"I smell gas," Mama would say,
and like sow bugs exposed to light
we'd scurry to every source,
possibilities of the moment.

What you remember is not all.
There are trickles from any waterfall
that seep unseen for years and years
before the inundation.

Too late is the implosion —
the embrace, the grasp,
the choices lost,
no longer a now.
The jolt of the impact
repeatedly sizzles:
Your life lies behind you,
gray ash, live coals.

*May 26-30, 2010*

THE HIDING BOY
(To My Brother, A.E.)

It was something he enjoyed—
the gray of early morning rising,
the secret passage down the stairs,
the pioneer tracks across the wet grass.

His small hands parted the forsythia sprays,
edged under the green splays of daffodils,
separated the long grass spears
at the base of the Japanese maple,
laying the bright-colored eggs in disguised nests
for the younger ones to find.

Damp morning air and grass stained him
as he loped, deft and concentrating,
big-eyed, button-nosed,
quiet as the cottontail he aped.

Now grown, a father, does he
still play the Easter bunny
rousing no sleeping tigers
in the long morning grass?

*April 1980*


GOING OVER

"It's just down the road a piece," the old man said.
She went trustingly, back fifty years,
and stepped into black,
the death of all colors;
the air stiff with it;
the houses, the streets imbued with it;
and a stench of the subterranean —
Coaltown, where she wasn't to be but was.

Her eyes absorbed too much,
the overflow pervading all her senses.
Half-drowned, she moved uncertain,
a strange dull twanging inside her ears.
Time crunched by on the cindered street.

Colors after that were never real.
She was always crossing from Kansas to Oz
over the rainbow bridge.

Now that the colors begin to mute ,
she knows all things lie
down the road a piece.
People and houses fade
and the tongue plays
stumblebum to the brain.

Yesterday's daisies
petal the intellect with lunatic fringe
just down the road a piece.

*Oct. 1992*


FEATHER DUST
(Remembering Daddy)

My nose prickled —
the unfamiliar dust,
the alien closeness,
that hushed expectancy
a foreign crowd emits —
pigeons, a legion of them
in a new coop built by my dad.

I watched him—
broad- shouldered, huge chest—
making a mash of grain in his mouth,
then carefully picking up a tiny squab
and introducing its beak.
I startled at the unexpected,
a bird pecking into a human mouth
accepting what was offered.

"This is how the little ones eat," he said.
"Their mothers refused them
because the move upset natural instincts."

He walked along,
repeating the gentle cupping of each orphan
until all the abandoned were fed.

*Jan.8-13, 2013*

## HIDE AND SEEK

I tear across
the open space,
then down to my knees
in a shadowed place.

Hushed feet come toward me;
I swallow a scream.
The shadow grows larger.
The dark is a dream

I'll never escape.
I'll be the first found.
I'll have to be "It"
and seek in the void.

I tremble,
leap up before I am tagged
and run for the base.
I'm always afraid.

"Home free," I shout,
touching the comforting tree.
The dark lies behind me.
I made it home free.

*Nov. 19-Dec. 1, 1994*


## SEEING THROUGH

Once, long, long ago, gazing upward,
I followed the progress of a car
bumping over the clouds, taking away
the man who had "died and gone to Heaven."
The sky held what I did not know—
who was driving, how long it would take.
For days I wondered, "Is he there yet?"

Has my vision changed
or is there enough substance
beyond the image of a child's eye
requiring no interrogation —
simply acceptance?

*May 14-18, 2002*

## LONG RANGE

Remember
how light leaked
through the whorled skin of frost
on the window glass,
isolating,
insulating;
how the milk frozen in its bottles on the porch
pushed the cream up into Doric columns
capped with a simple cardboard lid;
how sometimes Mama would slice it off
and whip it later for a special treat;
how the little gas heater burning blue
and the oven, its door kept open,
pumped warmth into the kitchen?

Here where seasons merely seep into seasons
and June scarcely differs from March
or August from November,
I long to shudder,
to breathe onto an iced window
and watch the dissolving,
to struggle into a heavy coat,
thrust on mittens,
and walk in the crackling air,
my nostrils pinching shut;
to feel the cold slowly taking me
nibble by nibble
until my heart beats in my throat,
my eyes glaze,
and my long walk is over.

FALLING THROUGH
(Hello, 2002)

I burrowed through the coats,
stumbled over the galoshes,
and hunkered quiet and small,
listening to my brother searching
in a game of hide and seek.

Shifting in the dark,
I tumbled through the closet—
surprised and splayed
on top of my parents' shoes,
under the dresses and shirts —
transported against my will
through a passageway
I hadn't known existed.

In this today,
a half-century gone,
I see myself,
still hugged in a ball
behind old trappings,
afraid to move
lest I drop off into the unknown,
forced to decide whether to crawl back
or emerge on the other side.

*Dec. 30, 2001*




IN THE LITTLE HOUSE

I trembled in the dark front room,
the night stealing the window,
the murmurs of the family far away.
When Daddy came home,
something would happen to me.

"Where is she?"  I heard him say.

Then he was coming  through the door,
huge against the sudden light
angled sharp as a knife.
I froze into the curtains.

One pinned moment and he closed in,
picking me up,
carrying me
into the yellow glow of the living room.
On his lap I sobbed and gulped,
splashing tears.

He sat silent,
holding me
until I shuddered away
the punishment of dark and isolation,
breaking into a thousand pieces against his warmth.

*Feb. 2000*


## INFANTILE PARALYSIS

We were caught in a prolonged summer,
the schools not open
when Infantile Paralysis reigned.

The worry of  parents was peripheral,
no more interfering than daylight
sneaking down behind the hills
before we finished our games.

Vacation became an endless playing
of Hearts, Parcheesi, and Monopoly
on a concrete slab
in the shade of our mulberry tree
for my sister, brother, and me
joined by  neighboring children.

"What's the sense?" my mother asked.
"They're all together anyway."

Although none of us caught that dreadful disease,
I sometimes think the long September
seized me, forever infantile
squirming futilely against a hidden paralysis.

*Feb. 22 - March 1, 1999*

## COMPOST

In newsprint lean and dark,
words ran. Between my hands
the killer bared blank eyes.

In the wealth of summer
in the bruising heat
he had dropped  the corner druggist
on the garbage;
driven twenty miles;
bought new clothes;
stowed the extra cash
in a Greyhound station locker.
He had hired a taxi
to come back home.
The roadblock stopped him.

Face-down in the spill,
his glasses gone,
they found him,
Doc, murdered.

In the quick moment
heat melts,
fat and slick.
Potatoes slab.
Egg sockets gape;
tin cans pulp gouged ends.
Grapes ooze slime.
The folded body
blades its bones,
dries with rust.
Against silence
a cricket saws its legs.
Day yellows in dull resonance
under a Van Gogh sun.

My father's eyes, gone to pine,
spoke over greedy earth,
acting against afternoon.
Dust particles lay on my tongue
like cockleburs. Doc!

Fall sun crushed vision.
The white under- belly
blossoms raw milk of maggot.
The summer flesh grows to earth.
In the compost grape, tin,
potato rime, glaze.
Only egg shells
shroud the heat of moment,
quick and fat.

*1960, Seattle*


HARVESTING

Crouched in that lush garden
carefully snapping off  string beans into a bowl,
I did not know that half a century later
I would reap the fruit of my mother's planting.

A continent away in the cool Northwest
with gulls and crows flying shadows over me,
I inhabit that chubby child's body –
damp with the heat,
tiring of the task
but not of the rich texture of the pods
rippling under my fingers.

The quivering waves of heat intensify
until the gathering is more dream than reallty.
Robins dare the earth close by.
Fat bees brush against my arms, snag in my hair.
The sun flattens on my head
as I carry the filled bowl into the house.
The beans, cooked al dente as we like them,
hold their jade color.
How few they seem
steaming on the plate.
Time was long in that hot garden.

I hunker down warm as July
in that ripened season—
careful of the tender vines—
gathering more than food for sustenance.

*Jan. 4-11, 2000*

OF HUMAN BONDAGE AND GOSSAMER WINGS
(For Gay whose illustrations bring it all back)

When I was small
the fairies carried leaves for parasols
and came to afternoon tea
in the shade of the mulberry tree.
They sipped nectar  from petal cups
and delicately sucked
honey straight from the comb.
When the sun rayed golddust paths
all the way to earth,
lighting their filigreed wings,
they drew together and fluttered up.
The light remained in soft diagonals.

I never succumbed to the charm of wings,
the exquisite freedom of those unsullied beings.
No kin to me:
I with scabby knees and bitten nails
and shoes toe-scuffed
who wanted only to move fast enough
to escape the ground and, wingless,
perpendicular to their shining path,
run on air, four inches from earth.

*Nov. 30-Dec. 5, 1995*

ONCE UPON A TIME

One by one the petals dropped
with "loves me, loves me not"
and jump-rope ditties sounded out
"Tell me the 'nitial of my sweetheart."

None of this was ever lost.
The child I was remains in me,
a piquant constant curiosity
divorced from common sense.

For should I jump that rope again
or pluck the daisy bare,
my heart would flutter—it's open season——
and I'd still believe the answer.

*May 18-29, 1998*

TERRA INCOGNITA
(Testing Stilled Waters)

Going down,
I hesitate on the last step,
my foot hovering
uncertain of the terrain.

What if it should be cinders,
the remembered crackling
from the substitute floor
put in long ago by my father?

What if the saddle traded to him,
who never owned a horse,
still hangs on the wall?

What if the shelves are filled
with nails, planes, wrenches,
Dap compound, paint?

What if the make-shift table
is lit with its single bulb
wired across the beams?

Would my dad be there
with his carpenter's pencil
measuring?

*Jan. 7-15, 2004*


PRIMARY SCHOOL

Nobody turns back the clouds,
brushes away the fog
to wake up morning;
not the crow
nor the chipping sparrow
pipping away atop the fuchsia.

The child of the 30"s
knows who can,
hearing the bottles clank
in the milkman's truck
sneaking down the street.

*July 21 -23, 2012*

## SEASON FOLLOWS SEASON

Back East in spring
morning comes suddenly,
the earth steamy with decay.
Apple blossoms sparkle,
daffodils flow downhill,
and winter is only the faintest cool kiss
at daybreak, evaporating with the sun.

And always Mom,
her hands gone loose on the sudsy dishes,
her eyes the blue of forget-me-nots,
stands transformed at the kitchen window,
dreaming of rich colors
still sleeping in the friable soil.

*April 5-6, 1995*


## RUNNING BETWEEN THE RAINDROPS

The midnight mirror shimmers
faintly lighted from the street
reflecting neither here nor prescience
nor present world nor time.
Myriad images swirl and whirl,
coalesce and separate.
Unpatterned in their constancy,
they permeate the veil.
She closes her eyes.

All paths are inviting, open,
the hills no longer dark,
the stunning sun welcome,
holding the murky scent of the creek.
The boat slides into the water,
the oars feathering, timed.
Finally the shss of movement
is syncopated, rhymed.

*March 15-20, 2011*

## ROUNDING OUT

I never could dance,
but I could run —
outrun the wind,
outrun the rain.
My feet were winged
barely touching earth;
my body tucked,
a projectile, impelled
through time and distance.
No one surpassed me,
not even the boy
holding title to state champ.

I run still now—
fields and houses and people
blurring peripherally,
time and distance
the welcoming arms.

*May 23-24, 2009*


## BEDROCK

I inched,
unfolding from the fetal position,
flexing my toes onto the stove-warmed rock
gestating between the sheets —
the rest of me rigid,
my nose a December icecap
protruding from the blankets
but my feet toasting in July.

How many times I woke
seeking nurture,
only to find a cold stone—
the life of it long ago gone into me—
and push it away with my feet.

*Oct. 28 - Nov. 17, 1998*

THE UNANSWERED QUESTION
(For Scott)

The long long afternoons
the spice of gardenia
in quiet rooms
a piano that blooms
in the living dark
the lacing of hours
with sibling talk
the giggles accompanying,
"Who dat up dair?"
the expected response,
"Who dat down dair?"
and the unanswered question,
"Who dat up dair
sayin' who dat down dair?"

I've stayed that child
of the warm afternoons
respun those moments
recreated those rooms
recalled all the voices
of sisters and brothers.
Yet over and over
all through my days
I've awaited an answer.
I've longed for the hour
that gives the response
to a query that's fair,
asking who are the who's
questioning the air.

*June 18-20, 2000*

UP BULLPUSH

Down in the valley where the river runs brown,
where the creek gets so shallow it's only wet ground;
where it Y's and it S's and it's finally naught,
you're up the holler, mister, up Bullpush Holler.

My mama has a possum filchin' food
from the tray for the birds she feeds through May.
"Catch him in a poke and let him loose up the holler."
That's what you do, what you do with a stray.

If you got a body that you want to hide,
if you wanna  go neckin' on the sly,
if you wanna pick berries you don't have to buy,
go up Bullpush Holler.

If you go up far enough, they say,
you'll have to come back the other way —
around ten mountains and twenty miles of track.
If you don't keep goin' you don't get back.

Who's that laughin' in his great black beard?
Who's that smokin' the houses gray?
Who's that brimstonin' the mountain water?
You might find the answer up Bullpush Holler.

*Jan. 9, 1967; Sept. 26, 2004*


STEEPING IN FLOWERS

Deliberately I seek the daffodils
against the long tomorrow.
By the fence west of the gate,
the curved walk begins with them,
there where barefoot impressions
by order of birth
fade away in the concrete.

I savor the sharp yellow sting
with eyes, mouth, nose;
and hear the silent trumpeting
from all the open throats,
an Easter sound
of pain then resurrection,
the round of life, the surge of faith,
the start of recognition.

It's spring again by heart,
the tiny-muscled intellect kept still.
All I was
again I am
at home with daffodils.

*June 8-20; 1995*

## AND ONE TO GROW ON

I hope my mother sleeps under the willow's
breath in that house, that earth-glad house
with so many rooms now tucked in for the night.
How once I moved through that universe
in the mirror-sharp terror of my youth:
ten rooms, two baths, two long halls
infected with dark, shadow, and creak!

My sister outgrew me. I was cast
into the vast outer space of another room.
Long, narrow, facing east, it knew
the rarer radiance of moon; the reassuring steps
of my father snapping quickly down
the snake-shaped walk; and the pale glaze
of streetlight through the branches of the locust.

My next room caught the tops of tallest trees,
the ripe black scent of coffee, and the throaty
warmth of Mom and Dad and the current baby.
But my last room owned the willow
where the wind's prayers cadenced.

Then house by house I moved away
from what was maiden-green and mine.

Now room by room I long for change:
Where is my "one to grow on"?

*Circa 1974, La Mesa*


## REVOCATION

The dark will rise from the river
and I will go home again.
The moon will slip through the curtains
and the shadows rein in
to their proper places in corners
where the night is gathering sleep.
The train will mourn down the valley track
coming back, coming back, coming back.

*April 10-20, 2002*

RESIDENT IMMIGRANT

The girl of make-believe
plopped stones into the creek,
listening to the swallowing gulp,
watching the circular ripples moving out.

Later she learned
to skip flat ones over the water,
cocking her head to throw
and to hear the sweet kiss of each landing,
but no discernible sound
on the final drop.

She wondered if those stones,
taken from the shore and tossed
alone in their flight,
uncertain of their destination,
alien in their landing spot,
were accepted.

*Jan. 23-24, 2010; Oct. 5, 2012*


WHAT'S OUT THERE

If you live in the mountains,
you know only that the sky
does not end at the treetops.
If you stay in these shadows,
you never know a horizon.
It drops into the unseen
on the other side.

I used to wonder
how anyone would get out of there,
but my mother knew horizons.
She fashioned from words and music
what lay beyond.

The years brought me a continent away,
to the coast, where the sky ends
and you know it.
There is nothing more of earth than water.

*Aug. 7-10, 2003*

## THE WINDS HAVE BLOWN OVER

I miss those winds that lifted me
on Mercury's heels to leave the earth;
but I'm taller than Mama's garden now,
a country away from youth.

How cold it was! I used to hide
myself up to my nose and sleep
the sleep of ancient queens beneath
my mother's opulent raccoon coat.

A frost as thick as pastry climbed
my windows as I slept. My feet
snugged up against a rock
I had warmed at the stove before night.

One wind sluiced through the windows, walls;
it sang, it purred, it cried and growled.
I dreamed of love and sable coats,
of troikas, bells, and someone's eyes.

One wind in a love of pure whirl
burst open my door on the night.
My heart thumped the size of my torso
and broke in the top of my throat.

I miss those winds that weathered me,
that turned me inside out;
that flung me wild and spilled me wide
across the continent.

I miss those winds that signaled change,
that stripped the leaves from autumn trees
and blew them at a winter moon
for twenty years. But I've spent that age.

*Circa 1965-66; Glendale*

## THE STILL-BLUE YONDER

I do not know what hopes I drew
from the long cool afternoon;
only that I dreamed alone
between two shades of blue,
shoulder-deep in Taylor Pond
until the sun dipped  low.

From the summerhouse my parents watched.
I heard my daddy say,
"She's all right."
But to this day I do not know
which of them really knew.

For even now six decades past
I seek no depths and take no risks.
But fanciful still I dream my dreams
in color as a child will do
and find myself in Taylor Pond
between two shades of blue.


## THE NIGHT BEFORE CHRISTMAS

I bordered on a little sleep
and raised my riots quietly.
Where was Santa with his sleigh?
Crossing the bridge from yesterday.

I jiggled in the tardy night
and arced my brows to resemble deers'.
But nothing stirred not even me
when the mulberry struck its antlers
against the house, against the roof.
Then suddenly it was driven hoof
and sleek of sleigh and bag of toys
and pumpkin-bellied Santa Claus.

Morning burst like a punctured moon,
painted the walls, uproared the stairs.
And there we stood all starched and solemn
at half-past six on Christmas morning.

*Nov. 27, 1974*

## THE STAR IN THE PALM

Kneeling alone in a field of frost,
I slipped my fingers under the crisp ice
and watched the stars disappear into my hand.
"A star in the palm represents talent,"
my mother once told me.
She had one, carved deep under the creative finger.
"I always thought," she said, "it was for the piano."

Rubbing the moisture into my palm
creased only with X's and Y's,
I remembered her small concerts
tucked between child care and chores,
the buoyancy of her body on the bench;
and music like fire
eating the walls and ceiling
until there was nothing
but a giant pulse of being.
And, I bodiless in those moments,
absorbing the full range of existence,
knew the universe for all time
through the light of her star.

Under the pale January sun,
my hands pocketed,
fingers curled to hold the warmth,
I knelt once more
and watched the stars go out,
grace note after grace note.

*Jan. 6-24, 1995*

## BIG SISTER
(June 29, 1927—Sept. 11, 2012)

It was not a dream
that traveling down
the long dark hall
to the safety of
my sister:
"Can I sleep with you?"
she, blanketed with dreams,
flipping back the covers,
I tucking in
shutting out the terrors
that ballooned in my room
two doors away.

I know it wasn't
because I still seek
blindly in the dark
for another share of her warmth,
her unquestioning acceptance
of frailty, of need.

*Oct. 28-29, 2012*


## BURNT OFFERINGS

You see them still
cracked dry with sun —
mud pies on the concrete step —
and wonder why you made them.

Even then you did not know,
disliked the ooze and boggy stink
you squeezed and shaped and patted,
the stiff and papery residue
drying on your hands.

There was no pride of achievement,
scarcely a moment of fun
in offering a nasty pretense,
accepting the false "yum yum."

## BACK COUNTRY

Years ago,
lost on a mountain  road,
we stopped at a tiny grocery
to ask directions.
The talk among the idlers picked up.

"Somewhere out there
they's an ol' cannon
from Civil War days."

"Who told you that?"

"It's out there all right.
Pa Pa always talked about it.
I figure he oughta know.
Him and his friends
nosed 'round for years lookin'.
Never could find it."

The talk went on and we did too,
dismissed by shifted shoulders
and a tightening circle.

Since then I've pushed through dense hills
looking for what was said to be there.
But in all the darks that followed—
light cut off  the way a mountain swallows the sun—
I never stumbled over anything lost through the years.

*June 7-13, 1999*

## A TONGUELESS THUNDER

I knew the ocean –inland– as one wave
that rose recurrent, taller than my house;
a phantom out of quiet drought, a taste
of bitter shining worm before my time.

The wave erupted fully formed; it walled
a horror in my throat. Down its soundless
thunder poured upon my mama on the beach.
Always the same, dream-border high it came
when I burned with fever as a child.
My mama, dressed in unknown black, sat at
my little table, stranded in her calm.
Her island disappeared without a sound.

Sometimes I break upon that split world yet.
I catch my breath on lightning during storms
and hold it over thirty years before
I hear the redemptive clap of thunder.

*Sept. 19, 1966*


## THREE SILLY SYLLABICS
## BLOOD WILL TELL

The telling blood steals
the sham of feigned acceptance;
paints the cheeks crimson.
Only the color-blind see
the true blush of innocence.


The throat, the wrists pulse
against the flattened fingers.
"Hmm. Not in balance."
The acupuncturist squints.
"This is most unusual."


He came from behind,
put his arm around my waist —
a complete stranger.
"June," he said. But, alas, no.
I could not be my sister.

*July 4-8, 2001*

THE REVIVAL

With a gloat in the throat and a wheeling spiel,
it was off to a golden grandeur.
Eloquence flashed and the cymbals crashed
while a woman fought the devil.
In her sharkskin dress which was molded by sweat
she swayed from her knees to her back.
The dim old drum blurred its rum-tum-tum
until the spirit came upon her.
Then out, chin; back, chin; out, chin; back;
face in the fervor of primate past.

     Winds in the morning
     and winds at night,
     blow my sins out,
     make me white,
     pure white.

A boy who was drunk every weekend came
through the door of the tent to repent and be saved.
The exhortations flew thick as wings.
"Brother, brother, get on your knees."
The spirit touched him
and his head went wild
and his shoulders jerked and his eyes grew blind.

     The wheel of the Lord
     it ground so small
     the revival kept going
     until the fall.

*Circa 1965-66*


THE ISLAND

is falling off in clumps,
tumbling in tufts,
breaking and shearing,
sifting and flowing
into the gnawing river
always hungry for more.

*May 5-9, 2010*

# BEFORE THE STARS FELL

Lillian was a horse of a girl, years younger than her flesh.
Often she leaned from the single-windowed upstairs room,
her plump arms flattening along the sill.
She played with us, with a fuzzy mothering
as if we were teachable dolls:
Our hair was coaxed to twirl around her fingers,
our plump legs restrained from swinging
when she held us on her lap.

Her mother worked, leaving her limitless and strange.
No one ever mentioned any father.

"Would you like to see stars up a coat sleeve?"

She stirred us up a magic, for they were there —
little flips of water flung down the rigid sleeve I learned later,
for I was always practiced on first, being only Next-to-the-Oldest.

Once she took me to her house to play at looking at things:
tiny wooden chests, miniature china dolls with stiff hats and ruffs,
glass medicine vials, and assorted cardboard powder boxes.
She laid them out upon the bed on a quilt of soft blue ships
permitting me to pick them up and savor one at a time.

Mama showed me blue-eyed surprise when I told where I had been.
She never let me go again
but not until last night, remembering
under autumn's clear unbroken stretch of stars,
did I know why.

*Nov. 14, 1966*

## TO MY SISTER

I would like a letter from you,
the lilt of your language apparent,
the darks and lights of your fancy
complementing each other,
the warm bloom of yesterday heavy
with the fragrance of today.

Write
that you lounge under summer clouds
naming the drifting shapes;
that you torment your tongue
with the bitter of nasturtium leaf.

Write
that when awkward as fledglings
we stood upright
on our own ends of the seesaw,
balancing the ups and downs
then timing the movements
to jump off together,
we were conjoined,
not just for those moments
but forever.

Write me
that out of this wilderness
the sun and moon may be contrasts,
that nothing is ever lost.

*June 13-14, 1998*

# TRUNK

## SERRATION

I heard you sleepless in the night
stumbling down the dark of days.
Your feet were clods of baffled earth
ringing paeans in a maze.
At last toward dawn silence hung
incumbent space between our doors.
The puppet strings of tired fate
dangled shadows of the noise.

Daylight anchored great gray eyes:
the clangor in you slept.
My quieted thoughts resumed their rounds
endless, unseamed, unchecked.

*1959, Seattle*


## RESTITUTION

Time is confounding,
bubbles across the brain
mesmerizing in their fragility,
in their stunning iridescence,
Tuesday hung over Wednesday
limp as a Dali clock.

The sky is cracking open
disgorging the yellow yolk of the sun
proud above the slurry,
on the calendar of March.

*March 19- 26, 2011*


## QUERY

Why does echo print its hurt,
still retain your laughter?
Shall all of life contain the dregs
or only the mourning after?

*1958, Seattle*

SEEKING THE GOLDILOCKS ZONE

Sometimes you close your eyes against the light,
softening the shards of thought too bruising illuminated.
Colorless, they lose their intensity, stripped to essentials
like bones exhibited in an X-ray.

Jeanne's still there, minus the yellow of her hair, the coral of lipstick;
wide-mouthed, giggling her joke as truth to serve her ends.
"She probably went home to get married," she had told him
when he asked where I was.
(I'd guess she loved the shock on his face.)

I never saw him again.

Fifty-six years ago and I, child-woman, denied the choice,
stand frozen, still locked in that nightmare dyslexia:
Why am I? Where do I go?

*Sept. 14-Oct. 15, 2010*


SONNET: THE WILLOW

Here willows slope like children's arms in sleep,
caresses curved to hold the pressing dark
apart from deeper depths of dark that creep
along the earth. Serene, alone, apart,
the willow dimly dreams of one it left
to time: a fair Ophelia, cruciate lain
along its narrow branches bridging death,
a palliative peace released from pain.
Now rimed with dust are eyes that knew with me
the cool mercurial qualities of time:
the quiet pride, each season's entity,
that melted into mountain's cloistered prime;
soft-stained with earth the mind that restlessly
taught me the shape of life beneath this tree.

*1959, Seattle*

## SUNDAY INDULGENCE

A chesty rumble
of thunder wakes the sleeper
who identifies
the sound and awaits
the fury of explosion,
the culmination,
the suspension of sound
before rain shatters against
the glass – the coda.

*Jan. 6, 2008*


## THE EDDY

November sneaks in
hoping to be winter
but autumn lingers
pouring its blue sky down
dissolving the hail.
Nothing is predictable.
The rosebush is carrying twenty buds,
yellowing its leaves,
drooping uncertain of desiccation.

Here is Mike telling us to wear
something loud, crazy with color.
A late salvo to Halloween
disappearing around the corner
or a salute to approaching Thanksgiving?

The in-betweens are with us
slithering snake-like into consciousness,
spitting out venomous  in rebellion.

Approaching the cusp of winter, we vacillate
more wary of acceptance than change.

*Nov. 4-0, 2008*

## THE MODERN

You were just someone
who came to dinner on Friday
night. I swallowed swords,
feeling the tip touch
my stomach the ten minutes
before you came. Somehow
the lining was never severed
until the Fridays came without you.

Now the end of the week
is tinged with rust. My stomach
knows no blade; my teeth
clamp no chill steel.
Meat and potatoes are fine.
I drink my wine
without fear of putrefaction
under the lip of your scorn.

I mellow like autumn fruit,
sleeping long and yellow,
curving toward forgetfulness.
The arc of the moon moves
Mount Rainier to mimic
winter dragons, New Year's breath.

My debts are paid. I sleep
lonesome with two pillows,
the hollow in my heart
where the wind whistles,
and the gnawing famine of Friday night.

*1959, Seattle*


## "THE LOON"
(Painting by Jacob Elshin)

Black motion of separate feathers,
beak that preys on air —
wind channels describe you.
That the unholy speed of your passing
should be eternal!

*1959, Seattle*

TIME OUT

Where is John with his shepherd's eyes
that held me in the flock?
And where are gentle morning suns
and pristine skies and untamed clocks
and wands of fairy godmothers?

I mourn their loss in lidded light
of day past four o'clock. Now spent
with bitter salt is flight
that cracks my calm with willful spite
and sends me back to harness what
reins in my heart to remember.

It rises out of summer
where the meadow narrows close
and mountains rise and turn their leaves
to let the autumn in.

The creek goes golden brown again
where early rain lets down its hair
as straight as sticks into its depths.
A chime rings there where water hits
on water decks. Lethal, lethal is
its charm, enchantment in a sound.

I lose my years, my matron-age,
become a girl again
and lean far out to listen
for that legendary pipe,
that distant scattered magic,
that rainbow-dusted lake,
the golden days, the green-pine years,
the apple bite of O.

Bell me, Pan or Piper,
once more, once more.

*Sept. 29, 1973*

SHORT-SIGHTED
(One-eyed Playboy)

An admirer of Moshe Dyan,
he sometimes wore a patch
over one eye.
True, he saw but half his world,
an uncentered vision
necessitating a constant turning
if he wished a panoramic view.
Otherwise, one peripheral
was the side of his nose.

*Oct. 22, 2000*


SPLIT WORLD

Sometimes I stumble into that split world
where dreams exist as they were dreamed.
I am washed with imagery,
eidetic pictures clear as rain
pouring through my wakened brain.

Seven times ten I'm still the same
as when the hollyhock became
my Cinderella gown;
and life, the other life, spun on
outside my enchanted circle.

For only a moment time held still
but the charm remained suspended:
Somewhere beyond
I'd find my prince
cloaked in the realm of shadows.

No matter,
for I was kissed by star dust
in the glow of a rosy moon;
could always be what I'd never be —
the reigning queen of the ball.

*Aug. 27-Sept. 18, 1999*

REGRESSION

I wrote you a poem once,
a tease of words
you couldn't possibly understand.
But I was a romantic —
thought you would look at me
with love for the effort,
that it would express me
without a stumble.

Now when I read
that forty-year old tribute,
I wonder:
Did I know so little?

*Jan. 10, 2000*

PROGRESSION

My grandmother fended off dying
with the back of her hand.
"It's Arthur," she said,
"on the other side of the brook
telling me 'Jump, Edie, jump.'
It's too wide I'm telling him."

Yet nothing is too wide for long.
The eye takes measure by mind and need.
The heart and lungs grow quiet, seek rest.

Hosts of stars erupt in sparkles
around the moon with its gentle smile.
Only the burble of the wind disturbs
and the flat white squawk of a gull
before night lets down its sheathe of sleep,
a welcoming fare thee well.

*Jan. 14-March 6, 2001*

## DECEPTION PASS

Downed by flat-soled feet,
drop of raw slate,
spinning shale, he clawed
from earth his desperate halt
two yards from boiling water,
whirlpools that stayed power
boats on three-quarter slants.
He surveyed yawning water,
pouching land, his friend
halfway between him and substance.
"Come on down!" he shouted,
rubbing his rawed hands.
"Let's fish!"

Space
emptied above him. Vulture
faces beaked from the bridge
two hundred yards overhead.
He thumbed his skinned palms;
eyed the tackle box,
gray malevolent companion
in the fall; and threaded himself
to challenge and practicality.

Rubbering
his toes for the ascent, inching
into shale that pebbled racing
slides beneath his weight,
he fed himself upward.
One quarter of the way he drew
the gaff from the tackle; hooked
into earth pads that shredded
crumbled, lessened to nothing,
but sometimes held a foot.
Curbed by the box, he tossed
it ahead. In slow upward
loops it rolled then swished
with sickening speed down the slide
to the rocks below. The faces
above gaped cold anticipation,
ice of spectator sportsmanship.

The boy squared with disaster,
clamping the handle of the gaff
in his teeth, shifting for a solid.
The gaff slipped, skidded,
caught earth and hung
desire on a ninety-degree
angle two yards beneath.

Above, the faces hissed,
seeing over his head
firm ground, slant-obscured.
No knowledge touched
him. No communication
pared his edge of space.
Time flaked off beyond
the felled tree, dried
gray, half unhinged.

He crossed a drift of shale
to five holds on substance:
feet, hands, and face
dug into crawling nausea.
He nursed soft green, turned
his eyes inward, dulled
his existence.

The ranger came,
a hoop of brown rope, edged
a circle around the hill, cozied
the rope over drifting slide.
From tree then to man he walked
the tow. The scramble over eternity
closed in great red-sweatered arms.
"Good show!" the audience roared.

*1959, Seattle*

## VILLANELLE FOR SEATTLE

My heart knows  love as reincarnate spring.
I sense its sprout in thrusts, abortive pain.
I know the season has no summering.

The city quickens: fruit trees blossoming
crisp parasols that suction in the rain.
My heart knows love as reincarnate spring.

Camellias petal-paint the earth. I'm wrung
with riot, pink of joy. Can I restrain
delight? This season has no summering.

Fresh hail ice-whites the thought of weathering
the budding season's onslaught to reline
the heart with love in reincarnate spring.

Wet winds brushtip the mind, stinging
the cloistered buds of other years open
to know the season has no summering.

Untaught imagination's weather-sprung;
the measured reason feels emotion's strain.
Whose heart knows love in reincarnate spring
can do without the season's summering.

*1959, Seattle*



## TRIBUTE

Cotton candy tree
with licorice limbs,
you fed me through the night.

*July 10-15, 2010*

SUSPENSIONS

So many things broken,
reduced to shards and shadows:
A vase, that crazed red of which dreams are spun,
I bought in a rare circle of peace,
defining it with my hands
for long round moments before deciding.
The Sylmar earthquake smashed it.

A Baby Ben alarm clock,
creamy white circled with gold,
that timed me from grade school
through years of teaching.
My first-born tinkered with it
so that it would  run
only if it were set upside down.

An afternoon, the bowl of the sky
swimming with sheep,
drawing me into its depth.
A voice: "It's four o'clock."

Forty minutes in a Chinese tearoom
ripe with tingling scents,
time and anticipation running out
over a cold  pot of tea.
You never came.

So many residuals
suspended timeless
like figures in an oil painting,
for nothing loved is ever lost.
Nothing is remembered broken.
Everything's remembered whole.

*Jan.22 - Feb.-24, 1999*

## THE UNHARVESTED

All I know
or ever knew
is afterglow.
The years from now
to four ago
are buds of promise
never open, hopes of heaven
made suburban.

All you are
comes back to me.
Reality
is in those pears
plucked from your tree
two slopes below the house.

How you blend with Bergman movies,
how you notch my hardened core!
Are you gathering blackberries
with your strong Norwegian hands
to hold for morning?

With what two-fisted
granite grace
you lift the fence
to free the face
of some poor cow
out of country!
My unborn, tight,
beneath my heart,
kicked once.

Morning came:
A tree grew in the fog.
Five jars of pears,
captives this early,
bloomed in your kitchen.

All down these years
you've held a hand to me.
The order of the universe
has not been mine to see alone.
Although I ate your vegetables,
canned your pears
to hold the trust intact,
autumn comes again too soon –
too late for harvest.

*March 26, 1965*

## THREE PORTRAITS

I

The familiar pungence
of you is strangely verbal.
Your eyes bruise
like a bird's call.

II

Frosted with pain,
your eyes war with
your emotions' debts;
outmarble your heart
hung on winter's
tip breath, imagination.

III

Your strange eyes deny
kinship. They burrow blue holes,
snow depths undisturbed.

I tread no labyrinth
to meet you, live quiet,
apart from being.

*1961, Seattle*

## VIGNETTE

Vincent Van Gogh
painted his shoes
in repose. Tribute

to two left
feet, they gape
open-mouthed

in the museum between
"Apples" and "Potatoes,"
fruits of the earth.

The tour-guide
projects a thank
God I

am not as he,
but I know
my Van Gogh.

"His beard seems red;
it isn't. The eye
sees what can't be.

"Actually it's green
paint dabbed
in short stripes

"that gives the impression
of red. His head,
"Self-Portrait,"

proclaims what
photography can't —
his mental outlook."

Who reads his art
knows lust for life
that makes truth

tired when aired.
Eternal drought
pocks the palette

of understanding when
canvas must be studied
to make red

green if it isn't.
Why decry
subtle unity?

*March 1959, Seattle*


TOUCHING WORDS

She wrote me the color of her heart.
I wept because I could not answer.
No silly combination of vowels and consonants
substitutes for presence.

How futile to attempt
to cross the miles with words,
pit failure against possible success.
Yet how disdainful to ignore
with seeming diffidence
a plea for affirmation,
a plea for recompense.

*June 9-12, 2006*

TANKA
(For J.T.)

You bleach dark, make bright
leach patterns of yesterday's
entities. I pause
to break my heart against you.
The scar of you covers night.

I marshal, conscious.
So little of you winters.
Truth stings, scorpion
from the shadow of your eye.
You wither bones of pretense.

Forever is ash
tomorrow; wind etches sparks
on the night. The flame
of your  impetus singes.
Your mind is a burning lash.

Now memory moves
on the morning; reflects me
by half your heart. I
bitter the stem of longing.
Blossoms impale on my pulse.

*July 1959, Seattle*


SYNESTHESIA

May is the color
you daub on your dream's canvas
after April's shock
of snow feathering tulips
and hail peppering daisies.

May has melody
so simple that you singsong
naturally in
iambic or trochaic
mimicking the heightened pulse.

*April 28-May 3, 2008*

## SUNDAY AT THE BEACH

He lay drunken
with beer and sun
in a sand hollow

while his wife
drowned in Lake
Erie, drunk too.

"Get up, Dad!"
his daughter, mottled
red and blue

with horror, screamed.
"Dad! Dad!
Mom's drowned!"

Her teeth were gray
in crooked lines;
her hair awry.

Her eyes were a child's
Dali nightmare,
terror-split

two ways:
Fatherless, Motherless.
Candor dies young

when fathers grunt
in stupor, sun
and beer-baked

on sandy shores;
when mothers drown
in narrow waters

among inner-tubed
tots, beach balls,
and life guards.

Candor dies young
when Innocence is scraped
from eyes too young
for resuscitation.

*Circa 1958-1961, Seattle*

## LATE AUGUST

Alone in the field
I'm waiting for more than light —
for the grace of wind
to loft the spent blooms,
spill them on new soil
where tentative they test
its nutrients,
settle or float on.

It will come,
that sweet breath of autumn
hazy with pollen
lazy with promise
to soften the dearth of blossom,
the imminent shroud,
the sting of winter.

*Aug. 30 – 31, 2008*

## NIGHT OWL

You cannot close the book on night
where fancy twirls in dances you have known.
You have not grown beyond the frame of yesterday.
You seek the moon.

Until you turn
and lift your face to living air
where flower and weed sift pollen dust,
hear thunder open its giant mouth
with strands of rain spilling out,
watch April split away from May,
the calendar bloom thirty-one days,
you will not know that
nothing crouches in the dark
unless you give it space.

*May 22-28, 2006*

SWAN SONG

Each dark the hush of winged strength
creases the lake. Each dark a swan song
recreates you fledgling human.
You spill flesh into feathers, ice the night,
crisp the contour of mortality,
Odette, pirouette of fragile magic.

Three times around circles Siegfried.
You flutter at his being, shiver at his eyes, his arms.
One moment on the quiver, you hover. Then the pact is made:
Love forever. Dawn mirrors in the lake
where your pattern drifts, again a swan.

Odile in your guise turns the prince into man,
eye-blinded. Her smile brushes your changeling lover.
He announces new betrothal, spellbound.

Triumphant laughter unseals your Siegfried's eyes.
Together, against the rising lake you seek
the old mirage death to lose deceit.

Now no bird wing of strength, no lake
of frost flutter the secret heart. No hunger tempers
the terrible truth: Enchantment is broken by love.

*1959, Seattle*




OCTOBER

Especially now October gleams
with frosty dew across the fields
and weeds blade silver under morning sun.
Dogs and people expand their senses
and sniff in the promises of intent
a chill north wind suggests.

It is time to hunker, sweep out the spent,
prepare for what is different.

*Oct. 26, 2008*


63

## UNDER THE SKIN

The crocus and I
have much in common.
Our mouths buttered with sweet
purse prolific kissings,
hiss when the wind turns.

*Circa 1958-1961, Seattle*

## REVERIE

I have been here before,
oars arrested in my hands,
my boat the anchor
to what I knew,
the sea reflecting
the sky unlimited
with its frothy spume,
its roiling surf.

Now, shore-bound,
feeling the chill,
I dissolve in the present,
my clenched hands empty.

*July 27- Aug. 1, 2010*

## NOVEMBER

November flows
in arpeggios,
leaves down the sky
in sullen waterfalls.
Final autumn chords
are soundless.

*1958, Seattle*

## THE WRITE-OFF

What spilled from the envelope
was only words,
the dried ink of expression
written yesterdays ago
from your Olympian heights
to my ivory tower.

Remembering too well,
I did not read them
but poured them back
into their vault.

In another forty years
I may do more than grimace
and say, "Ah, there's the rub."
I may read them—
and laugh.

*Jan. 4-7, 2001*

## IN THE BACK YARD

the night wind left
a shred of black plastic,
a crow's feather,
a torn roof tile,
a magazine page —
easy enough to gather,
to consign to a trash bin.

In the morning there are always leftovers:
the first- grader crying outside the door,
the second-grader lost on a strange street,
the early blossoming shame of the sixth-grader
overhearing a boy's smart-alecky observation—
all the smacks of childhood that keep on scarring.

*Sept. 6-23, 2012*

## THE RIDDLER

I kept offering you answers,
poems sweeter than June mornings
in West Virginia with the sun crawling
in the window silent as a burglar,
the white net curtains still as fear,
the walls yellowing through them.

I was always telling you how it was with me:
I held the sun in my lap
and knew that God was beautiful.
I could hear the worms slithering
over the concrete seams of the brick path,
seeking the good earth.

But you, you insisted
that I talked in riddles
so that finally whatever there could have been
dissipated like valley fog.

Clear-eyed, I squared my shoulders
through all those tomorrows
that only echoed your response,
with the romantic side of me
hoping it would be different,
the realist knowing it wouldn't.

*April 7-15, 1997*


## RESPITE

The harsh boggy call of crows
erases the dark from the day.
All of tomorrow rushes in
too soon for contemplation.

Far better this inundation
than the slow insomniac seep
of hours by minutes by seconds
that cripples anticipation.
I have stolen only one moment,
stripped bare of its clocked time,
to be lifted unmoored from this body,
to exult in the element of air.

*March 25-29, 2009*

JANUARY I

Concealed in an imaginary field
where dry stalks rattle
and the night wind hums
through the quills of the firs
I shall hibernate without longing
in warm drowses.

*Dec. 29, 2006 - Jan. 4, 2007*


JANUARY II

Bright Polaris punctuates the dark,
the clouds seesaw with the moon,
the old year dwindles,
the new one trembles,
anticipation fluttering the senses.
The blue of the heavens
keeps swallowing the gray.
January has two faces.

*Dec. 31, 2006- Jan.  4, 2007*


DITTY

I marked this morning yesterday:
The sun should touch there first.
Had I been nature's tender
that plant had died of thirst.

*1958, Seattle*


COCK-EYED: PRIMED TO KILL

A virago, a termagant —
with one cock of the eye
she had him,
and his age of dissent was over.

*April 11, 2003*

## SHOCK-PROOF

Dark disappeared
in traction's fetters,
cloying my limbs.
Ice packs, double-
weighted, marked
time in melting
hours. Needled
pain-killers
quartered days.

Nights differed.
Pain performed
blue-eyed aerials
on rope pulleys;
broke in silent
yellow laughter
along my spine.

At six o'clock
sun over morning
bleached my bones'
hidden abscesses
bark-white.
Encoffined, plaster-
limbed, I strove
for toes in familiar
movement to prove
my leg existed.

Sister of Mercy
with eyes like Lincoln
coins, crisped
white wings,
starched sympathy
in before-breakfast
trespassing. "September
Morns" she called
us in bathing hour.

Food moved mouthward.
Eggs turned sausage
between thrust and entry:
Mind and sight
over matter beyond
recognition.

I looked,
saw, knew
death laughing
in light was not death.

*1959, Seattle*

## INTERMISSIONS

You lie there folded precisely, like an envelope,
the contents unknown until opened.
The scalpel slices, the doctor reaches in.

Willing or not, you are always being parted
horizontally, vertically, temporarily, or forever.
Someone is always there ready to extrude.

Violation is not a pretty thing,
the body isolated in time,
the mind away in some anteroom
separated from memory.

Afterward, the spirit flails
seeking the lost time,
as subject to interpretation
as an ink blot.

*March 7-8, 2009*

## THE DROP-OUT

Bonnie kept her notebook
open; her fingers nimble-quick
to jot down every spoken
word, to savor every quirk
of fact or fancy. Bonnie's eyes
like shallow seas lapped the fringes
of her peers. November bleached the pattern.

Bonnie's face grew blossom-white.
Her father died. Her fingers boned
yet tighter to her pen.
She missed assignments,
failed exams. Her eyes wore puckered
seams. Still, she kept her notebook
current, filled with facts, not dreams.
A December morning brought the change.

Bonnie came, a smoke-wraith on the air:
"I'm getting married. Here're my books."
A diamond trembled on her finger.
The eyes kept asking, seeking
more, like open cups of thirst.
Her lip was tucked beneath her teeth.
She drew a short dry breath.

"What is it, Bonnie? Couldn't you wait?"
She shook her head, a silent no,
then drew her notebook to her waist
and warmed the bulge below.

*1965-66, Glendale*


## AUGUST

The roof has captured the moon
and is slowly snaring the stars,
but the sky immediately above my head
swirls the reflected light.

*Aug. 22-24, 2012*

BEFORE DARK

When I once was whole, in my early twenties, the evening accepted the bubbles I blew from the steps with a plastic pipe my brother had given me. Just enough light to see them loft and break in weeping rainbows on the rocks. Just enough light to see the house next door worn to its nubbins where the old lady lived alone. ("She invited you in?  She never lets anyone in her house.") I accepted her courtesy, bred in the blood. She had been a pianist, the room crowded with stacks of music and hundreds of leftovers from life. "I want you to have this," she said, putting "A Mother's Prayer" into my hands. She was the last of the real ladies I had known so many of —and  fading, as glorious as a sunset.

*Oct. 22-26, 2003*

BRIDGING

Nothing can hide the bridge,
its span dull pewter in moonlight.
I walk with wings, the edge given,
alert to headlights for I'm in flight.

Fearful that that man will follow me,
I make myself invisible. I disappear,
become each rail I pass, ending
at the county line, the crossing over.

Ahead is home, two long miles.
Safer now, I can leave the roadside,
fade out of sight, and walk the rails —
the time mine, the river running wide
scant yards away silent as I am silent,
furtive but there, its scent green and brown.

Forever the divide treacherous and serene,
the dark diffuses as the first lights appear.

*June 21-28, 2009.*

## THE MISFIT

There were some guys who claimed you right off,
who thought more than felt their dark philosophies;
who scorned your companions
held together by laughter and acceptance
based on long acquaintance.

I do not think that they were wrong
— I was after all a newcomer —
but that they singled me out
because they wanted an audience for their superiority.

*March 16-28, 1999*


## RECOLLECTION IN COLOR

Light sieves through the curtains,
a coastal gray resurrecting no color.
Even the raindrops lack iridescence.

The palette of memory opens
umbrellas flowering red and violet.
Without one, you and he,
disproportionate in height,
struggle to run in step.
Hands clasped, you duck
into an unlit storefront,
close together, laughing.

Perhaps now
in this newly glossed world?
No, of course not.
He is too careful;
you, too shy.

Neon signs sizzle orange and green,
headlights peer yellow,
rain silvers down the gutters.
But nothing holds light
like the blue of his eyes.

*Oct. 29-30, 2003*

THE SILENCE OF THE WOODS

The Douglas firs have danced all night.
You can tell in early morning
by how they lean into each other
with the rhythm of spent lovers,
trunk pressed to trunk, half-slumbering,
their roots entwined.

*Dec. 9-11, 2006*




AUTUMN TRANSPLANT

Fall slips onto the calendar
and melts beneath this sun.
I long for the turn of seasons,
the frost of autumns gone
to earth with leaves like crispy peels of June.

Every October brings to me the scent
of pumpkin, mince, and frost. The hollyhocks
have spent their bloom; the dahlia heads are bled
to gray. At night, the flesh of winter flakes
and frosts a ground of wrinkled furrows. Cats
and birds wear sharper tails for twitching chills
away. Meows and cheeps have thinned with the cold.
Even the barks of dogs rip short and harsh.
The mountains are three-dimensioned Seurat,
their leaf points gone to blurs.

The years have grown, pinched off my youth;
denied my rights of visit.
Yet, still the seasons crackle, lilt, and spin.

No winds from Appalachia can ice
a season's charm. No midnight chime can break
its spell; nor footmen turn again to mice;
nor Cinderella make a dream of ashes.

*Oct. 19, 1965, Glendale*

PORTRAIT

How like you
that fuchsia splash
of your scarf,
your lipstick,
your nails
shouting, "Look!"

How like you
the gorse,
its yellow language
gorgeous in its bloom,
and underneath,
the barb.

*April 1-2, 2010*


BUTTERCUP SUMMER
(For Linwood)

"You like butter?' he asked.
The cousin I knew
for twiddling his thumbs
thrust a buttercup under my chin.
"You do," he said, explaining that
the color reflects.

The years are long since,
but this summer buttercups flourish.
My neighbor has them massed
under his garage window.
They trickle through the fence
separating us.

I hold them in the summer of my eyes
as I do the boy who held one under my chin.
A singular picture of him
is in the family archives,
solemn and knowledgeable.
He died at sixteen— a heart attack.

*Aug. 6-10, 2008*

## APARTMENT HOUSE FRONTAGE

Seattle's seven hills are pared
and used to bolster pride.
Stones are thrown before each house
flaunting countryside.

The yellow-throated daffodil
howls from top-right corner;
the pink-blue heather gathers,
spits defiant stars;
sixteen purple tulips bulge
in pompous violence.
The earth is raw with rupture.
Rocks are recompense.

*April 1960, Seattle*


## BERRYING TIME

Some nights the lilac sharpens scent:
Old grief comes out of hiding.
The earth, the sky are both brown wounds,
the berry bush is blooming.

Just fifteen years ago this fall
your song broke from the dark. It turned
the night wind's pattern somersault,
erupted echoes in our blood.

Then off you went to wine the earth
on someone else's hill. You downed
us with your dying, Pete — your youth
like wild tart berries broken, spilled.

You downed us with your dying, Pete —
your youth splashed on the slopes
like great red globs of strawberries
that stumble in our throats.

We wore the silence, our habits set.
Marge drank, John moped, Jim sang.
But in the evening just at dusk
we mulched the berry beds for spring.

*Circa 1974*

APRIL

Were  my senses muted or is this
spring's first flock of wild geese
spinning a skein of hieroglyphics
raucous against the damp sky?
Their dedication to order—
leader and led,
pattern and sound—
pricks a slumbering kinship
to childhood: I could fly
if I used my arms for wings.

In this grand sweep
of sound and movement,
this wildness born of instinct,
time stops and a century is nothing
but this exultation of moment.

*April 14-17, 2011*


FLIGHT FROM FAREWELL

Your face was willed slumbrous
in the pressed warmth of day;
your eyes like stilled spring woods
drew me near, alert.
Strange how your presence has strength.

My hands betray me.
The coffee cup cuddled close,
the cigarette curled quick into ash.
Yet you note nothing
except what I do with words,
pale syllables left in space,
mute medicaments.

So careless, you, through impulse moved.
You may have tendered a mocking "E"
to ring discordant through eternity.

You never knew in that detached myopic state
that compunction bred compassion too late.

*1959, Seattle*

SEATTLE I

Soft-shelled autumn leafs
silence to the earth: Morning
is a blue-sieved dream.

Your late-valentine eyes,
sleep-fringed, hold tides of quiet
that waking lose me.

Love synonymous
with you, changeling on morning's
doorstep, startles the heart;

gives moment-measure
for longing, muted mulling;
refashions lost years.


SEATTLE II

Morning becomes time
found again in present loss.
These tactile hours spine-

finger erring nerve;
reline each tardy contact;
hone the numbing year.

Shaken by the start
of day hues, censure-bitten,
I pose cyclamen

lips in loose fresco
to warm my memory by.
Every eight o'clock

time-anchored roots stir
June to latent blossom,
flowering in the heart.

*1960, Seattle*

IN RETROSPECT

This anchored year I give you:
the broken face of time
kaleidoscopic memories
a summer's anodyne.
Sybil-tongued oration
mute-mouthed syllogy
staccato
legato
fitful harmony.
Elasticized momentum
anaesthetized relief
cogent, gnomic impress
synthesized belief.
Misologistic laughter
hiatus-harbored pain
nuances of nothing
allocated plane.
Mutual sustentation
sprite to sprite — what fun!
No more dream-dyed mornings
all that's done's undone.
Yet some peeping magic
is still unstained by art:
It's woman's whole existence,
of man's life yet a part.

*1959, Seattle*


ISOLATION

The leech draws blood,
but painlessly.
It does not turn
red, pink, or blue —
giving the lie to
you are what you eat—
but stolid, the color of pus,
it clings to its prey
with the air of finality.

*Aug. 9, 2004*

## JUNE MORNING, VICTORIA

Morning becomes.
The breath of birds is raucous
in the moving east.
Flower tendrils trace
night's spare edge
in live frescoes
basket-hung above the door.

Victoria crispens:
Power-gliding gulls
glow gloss in the sun,
narrow roads ribbon
to the botanical oblivion
of Butchart sunken
in the Country of the Blind.

*July 8, 1958*


## JUNE MORNING

Always there is some small sorrow
leaching salt into hidden wounds,
inoculating the blood with grief.
Or not?

A bird, red-bibbed, unidentifiable,
perches fleetingly in the pine,
and decisively wings away.
The mourning dove ceases its plaint,
woo-hooing in flight.

I absorb the morning
inhaling the tardy spring;
flutter and preen expectant
to know if I can fly.

*June 17-20, 2010*

## SONG OF SUMMER

The blind boy swimming in the river
cried, "Where's the shore?"
The laughing answers burned
his lids that knew no light.
"Please," his voice receded,
hiding desperation. Against
his shallowing consciousness
the voices broke in bubbling laughter.
The newspapers said he drowned.

*1959, Seattle*

## MID-SUMMER

The moths blossom on the night.
Their wings murmur idiot
perceptions, ashy glimmers
of truth. Flocking and fluttering
near the light, hovering,
sputtering on a single spot,
they invite death by making
themselves its brown suggestion,
cacophony in the quiet.

*1960, Seattle*

## IMPREGNABLE

The music sleeps
under the hands,
the piano keys,
and between the strings
in its own Helicon.

*April 2-4, 2010*

## INVITATION TO THE DANCE

I think I've been here before
where the cake cries Eat Me
and the bottle whispers Drink Me.
I believe I was under the table,
small enough to be stepped on
until I found courage in a label.

Again and again
I consider the invitation,
rise to it if warranted.
I may grow or be diminished
but stasis is not an option.

*2007; July 5, 2008*


## RENAISSANCE

Nothing but rain
quiets this pulse,
heavy, gray
absorbing moments
and movements.
Impulses tremble
on the edge of being,
fall, die
in pure purples
of dissonance.
Sleep mocks a
compact existence,
shaken, disturbed.

Elusive is the growth
to dawn's glad eyes,
robins' voices,
honey-ed winds,
and the simple pride
of the crocus
baring its heart
to a spring
it does not remember.

*1959, Seattle*

81

## THE STEAMBOAT CAPTAIN

His stomach protruding, extending to his chin,
couched sixty-nine years of reality.
Apart from serenity he could not be:
The Ohio had nurtured, intrigued,
soothed him from fifteen.

His watch face bore his name;
its chain, a pilot's wheel;
his heart, a stamp of divinity,
identification with mankind.

*1953-54*


## FALL

Autumn-fettered
heart-in-hiding,
leaf-tuned
your spirit
flit-turns,
finds
its current,
sites
its landing;
crumples.

*1958, Seattle*


## HOME COUNTRY

The night splinters
I draw deep breaths,
enter the old land
where chance and adolescence
knew me ten years ago.
There I worry your remembered smile
into being again,
seasoned with the spring
of West Virginia.
The trains keep running,
splitting rails.

*1959, Seattle*

TUMBLEWEED

When time is measured
my heart grows lean.
The dusky burrs of crickets keen
and all the flashing fronds of green
prick the end of spring.

The wind will push the night away.
Holding still for dawn to come,
I see the walks and houses bloom
like spectral promises. From the tomb
of spring's spent flowers, summer rouses.

*Winter of 1978; May 14, 1997*


PETERSBURG, VIRGINIA
(Displacing the Penny on the Glazed Eye)

Not with the long-dropped weapons
rusted to mere impression in the blood-rich soil
nor with bones or flesh,
but across the field in the evening air
men still move in the pattern of war.

None fall—no clash of arms, no shriek of pain,
no living horror, no cowardly shame
in the forward rush.
The battle endless, the final thrust
is played as was the first.

*June 15-17, 2001*


WEDDING RECEPTION

I see you, half-drunk, your voice unnaturally loud,
your arms waving about – and know a leftover shame for you.
Your parents have made themselves invisible;
your brand new wife is lost somewhere in the room.
Your crowd gathers en masse about me
exchanging pleasantries and laughing
as if they were my friends.

*March 2009; April 1-4, 2010*

## NO SENSE OF DIRECTION

Once I wanted to see
if he were there
in the old Pioneer Cemetery.
It was where he belonged,
but I could not find him.
I longed for a sharp
intuitive moment
that by its strength
would lead me
to where he was
going to dust
beside his forebears.

Once long ago I looked
for a certain Catholic church
(though I am not Catholic)
for hours in the early night,
but I could not find it.
I longed for the sanctified dark,
a place to hide in prayer
where if God touched me
in solace
no one else would know.

The mystery of seeking
without finding
plagues me.
A friend said,
"Maybe you weren't meant to."

That opened one door
but shut all the others.

*Jan. 11-12, 1999*


## TRANSMOGRIFICATION

I tossed a slug onto a tree,
a trowel-thrust unthinkingly.
Did it wonder where am I?
I never knew that I could fly.
If I've grown wings instead of feet,
I'll learn to land where I can eat.

*Aug. 11-17, 2008*

## TEA-READING

I have set my teacup down
and drowned in memory of your eyes,
the swimming brown beyond my depth.
But I would be more careful now
to seek an answer waiting there,
to catch once more a shorter breath
than I am likely to.

*Jan. 16-17, 2001*


## SPACED OUT

Nothing that you said
seared me. Instead
it was the flatness of your eyes,
the dropped shoulder,
the intake of breath;
and how the silence stung
growing large enough to flood my chest.

It was how you wouldn't meet my eyes
and the ease with which you settled in your car,
all like the last frames of the film rolling out;
and then dark
and quiet
and the rooms to which I returned
stretching wider than the night.

*Oct. 1996; Jan. 1, 1997*


## STILL LIFE

A little time is now
for words to bloom
in the mouth, the ears,
the nose, the hands,
and in that cyclopean eye
that marshals them
as synchronous.

*May 23 –June 5, 2011*

OUT OF SLEEP

Out of sleep the tissues burn
cold. How old these faces of night!
Slat-eyed day peeks out of turn.
The dark slips inside crookedly.

Day stretches to take the sky:
Somebody's child is weeping,
the peony's scarlet bursts on the eye;
an ancient wind is creaking.

Time knocks sharply in the skull.
The bones are prismed light
that arc a separate darkness
bartering over price.

Decision splits the brightest scar
the active mind can burn.
The seam of man is Harlequin
sutured by the Divine.

*1960, Seattle*


TO FEBRUARY
(For B.)

You season my senses,
you wuthering spring,
gusting, gathering whirlpools,
deluging quiet corners.
You rouse giant March,
voicing the night
that lifts my edges,
stays my willful caprice.

You sift through velvet dawn,
gathering the April color
of this daffodil
that blooms in my breastbone.

*April 1960*

THE MILKY WAY

If you wished upon the same star that Linda did, maybe you'd get what
Linda already had plenty of — fashionable clothes, beauty-parlored hair, a
house all polished wood inside, and boys, hanging around like servants.
"Hey! Let's both wish on that one!" "No," Linda said. "That one's mine."

*Oct. 14-15, 2004*


INTERIM

Midmorning— the stillness in the garden,
the gradual somnolence of transition to fall:

Alien kingdoms of mushrooms
rise from the needle-crusted earth —
some ecru, some orange, some brown
with yellow undersides crinkled and curled
like old leather Brogans.
Miniature rain globes trimming the pines
suddenly fall in long silver slices.
Spiders have spun their gossamer palaces
over the drooping grass.
Pale with sleep the sun
rays paths through the fog.

*Nov. 2-13, 2010*


SCARECROW

I am a figure of fun.
Even the crows pecking
at the straw blades of my hair
caw-haw in derision.

The wind balloons my sleeves,
scrubs the rope belt into my stomach,
sifts dry sand into my socks.
If it weren't for the broom handle
that supports my backside,
I'd wrinkle right down to despair.

*Aug. 27-29, 2010*

SEPTEMBER

Autumn is an opiate
that dulls the summer's spring.
Each antiquated season
needs memory's mellowing.

*1958, Seattle*


LEARNING CURVE

What if the table's too tall,
the chair  too wide,
the bed too short,
the shelves too high?

Do you keep looking, like Goldilocks
(who was fairly fortunate in finding
that one out of three fit),
and take what belongs to another
because it feels good?

Do you tuck yourself in,
relax until the usurped arrives,
upends you, and opens your eyes
to the surprise that  you can't fit
when you're in the wrong place?

*Dec. 28-29, 2004; Aug. 17-19, 2005*


UNRELATED HAIKU

You gave me many-
colored answers. Each one plucked
blossoms from my eyes.

Daily, beauty buds
the eye. Spring marries winter
outside my window.

Raindrops like quiet
colts alert the mind, carving
footprints on the night.

*1958, Seattle*

## A CLEAN SLATE

It's all right to slay your dragon
but the mind does not accept
piercing flesh
letting blood
stopping breath.

So, you think of it as paper—
cut
rip
crumple
without the sting of fear,
the cringe of guilt.

The remnants can be burned,
the char betrays nothing,
and the smallest wind
can scatter every trace.

*March 28 - April-2, 2006*


## GRETEL REMEMBERING

In the dark woods
with no semblance
of the trail,
no crumbs for comfort,
for direction,
there was the garden path
blooming richly,
a tickle of invitation,
leading to the house with
no locks and no keys.

The price for the knowledge
was paid long ago.
Safe places have locks
to keep you out.
To get in,
you need the keys.

*April 8-10, 2011*

FOR THE SEASON

Seattle-cherry-
blossoms in February.
My East Coast eyes long

for winter yet: frost
crawling stairs, staining glass dark.
Pink petals sprout crisp

ribbed spring, inverted
parasols cupping, warming
Ohio's ice blooms

alive in the heart.
Mornings mesh, memory-test
snowbud heritage,

the darker prelude.
Wish dies. The mind mirrors what
lies upon the heart.

*1959, Seattle*


HEAD-ON COLLISION

Twinned lights beaming at her,
dark surrounding her,
she asked aloud,
"Are you dead?"

In between being and not,
her spoken "No"
negated doubt,
affirmed position,
reflected time stopped
by her broken watch crystal.

1959, Seattle

## A LITTLE SOMETHING

A moment's breath for sorrow,
an affirming sip of rue;
immersion in a dewdrop
the sun shines through.

Double arcs of rainbows,
quadrupled pots of gold;
a folded bud the promise
of tomorrow's scented rose.

Hope taken by the spoonful,
three stars on a moonless night;
light scalloping the hilltops,
the gift of second sight.

*July 27 –Aug. 19, 2004*


## FEAR OF WATER

Swimming,
I could always see
the shadow of my body
under me,
fish-like
trailing golden strands,
enticing me beyond my depth;
suggesting that the best of me
was living under water;
that if I'd cease
to move at all
I'd find myself
as I began.

But fear was stronger
than the sparkling lure–
inhaling death by invitation.
I sought my depth
on solid earth
beyond the reach of water.

*Sept. 24-28, 1999*

## AGAINST ALL ODDS

She did not die
no tomb confined
no stone confirmed
yet every cemetery
whispered, "Cheat."

*1959, Seattle*

## DECIDUOUS IN DECEMBER

Each new outburst fails to thrive
and slowly drops its fruiting down.
What nips it in its seeming promise,
stifles growth so casually—
the disproportionate harmony
of wind and rain and kiss of frost?
Or, is it that the tender wilts
with a let-it-be philosophy?

*Dec. 11-14, 2012*

## CORNERED

On this short afternoon
don't find me
wedged in a corner
reading a book of poems
to experience vicariously,
avoid introspection.
I will be negated.

Poets know
erasing flesh from bone,
exposing strength in structure,
that constants will comfort.
The light and dark,
warmth and cold—
constants will pain.

*Feb. 10-20, 2011*

## THE NATURE OF MAN

Rocks guillotine the earth,
severing man's planting.
The raw red tulip heads
bobble in their tumbrils.

The tooth of beauty rags the wind.
Rain slits the patterned furrow
where man's transient blossoms
barb the soil he borrows.

*1959, Seattle*


## CONNECTING

See what the moon has done —
painted a tree in its own hue,
attaching it to earth
on a doubled trunk.

But looking again, I see
it is not to earth it clings,
but from its own shadow
springs upward —
effervescent with light.

*July 8-12, 2010*


## JUNIOR PROM GARDENIA

You lie with yellowed pages
and crumbling leather
on a folded sheet of shredding paper.

Neither scent nor color can resurrect;
nor can I in retrospect
recall a single moment.

*Feb. 14, 1998*

FRONTS

Reborn red-leafed, the rose
pushes out from old roots,
wary of the dead branches
with their still-lethal thorns.

Its neighbor, the purple smoke tree,
follows the same survival tactic
busying itself with birth,
inching away from its parent.

But nothing prompts the azalea
to reproduce, having spent
so much glorying in its flowers
that once is the culmination.

*May 12-14, 2011*




A SLEEP BALM  FOR WANDERERS

I smile at the implication,
rub as directed
a bit of it onto my temples —
oil of bergamot, ginger, rosemary,
lavender, and Balsam fir —
an infusion to enhance sleep.

But why the badger,
whiskery, twitchy,
long-clawed, rodent- eradicator?

Keeper of night in its place?
Ah, that's it.


*May 6-27, 2005*

## APRIL IN SEATTLE

The sun like flowering snow
blossoms late afternoon.
Surely this is spring.
The air a forgotten promise,
provocative, burgeons
in layered depths.
Each spring until I die
I die each spring
measuring the reincarnate.

*1959, Seattle*


## ENIGMA

That corridor of one breath
between sleeping and waking,
an eternity of suspension.

"I'll buy your dust,"
a thin wire of sound
in my ear, uninflected,
halfway between voiced and whispered.

"I" who?
"buy" when?
"dust" which?
I waited, knowing it was for nothing.

That was years ago,
but the thrum of the words endures,
my questions remain unanswered,
and I fail to understand.

*Feb. 12-14, 2009*

ART STUDIO CURATOR

He showed us
that dark was light
without electricity.

"See this early Tobey.
It's dark in light.
It's light in dark."

He smirked at the duality,
hawking the unexhibited;
his words the scythe of death.

How many live creations
died in this room?

*1958, Seattle*


REASONABLE

Once you came to my door
and I did not answer.
Sleep-drowned,
I had left sanity bobbling
behind me in another room.

*1961, Summer*


CHOICES

He told his mother,
"I want to be a railroad track when I grow up."

If I could choose,
I think I'd be
the moon's attendant star.
In the splendor of her wake,
I'd spend my hours cruising clouds
and dodging constellations.

*Jan.29 - Feb. 4, 2007*

## FACING UP

At the peripheral
vision creates what it
cannot see,
a fanciful, frightening
nonentity.

The brain shouts, "No,"
forcing the head to turn
to what was half
grotesque
becoming wholly so.

*April 2011*

## YOUR BIRTH DAY

Fashioned from
the borders of seasons,
this day gropes,
thrashes, yellow-fists
into morning's clock;
cockily faces the universe
with a lop-sided grin
from within.

*1958, Seattle*

## LITTLE ENOUGH

The slide to winter
comes with sun frost on the grass
silver lace on green.

Individual
dampened windows face the world,
blur the final blooms.

*Nov. 15, 2004*

THE GREEN YEARS
(For Caroline)

Rose scent from a cardboard square
titled "Essence of June" —
If I inhale, I recreate an afternoon
behind my apartment in Waukegan.

Sunning on grass, we laid our plans
to go out where the young West ends,
Seattle, Washington.

Possessions so divided us
that I by car and you by bus
saw the country separately, omnivorous
as young pups eating the landscape.
I missed your oohs and aahs and gasps;
mine are quieter testimonials.
Once there,
dominated by Mount Rainier,
I lived in the dorm
and you in town,
buying horse meat unaware
that it wasn't cheaper hamburger.

How we exulted everywhere,
corrupt as cannibals
feeding on an alien flesh,
strange yet nourishing.

We stayed close while I taught school
and you continued at the U.
Often I brought you home for dinner.
How you whooped and yelped over
the Russian Army Band Chorus,
a record I bought to flush my senses.

I married.
You were graduated,
taught out of town then went to Europe,
marrying someone there named Manuel
in Lisboa, Portugal.

For twenty years we exchanged at Christmas
until my gains became my losses.
Somewhere in the scroll of years
your latest address disappeared.

I miss your turn of mind for fun.
There are no more hurrahs from Caroline.

*Nov. 5-12, 1995*

# BRANCHES

CONJUNCTIONS

Here is profusion at its best —
purple lobelia massed at the juncture
of two drab roads.
In the swoon of color I make no decision.
Sensation absorbs thought.
I burble in remembered fields
floating with daffodils,
flooded with tulips
cresting with seas of dandelions.

Here at this intersection I accept indecision,
knowing that the road not taken exacts its toll,
the other awaits its due.

*April 27- May 11, 2008*


REALIZATION

A milder sort of schizophrenia
afflicts my derring-do:
I cope with kids and time and self;
I cannot cope with you.

*Feb. 29, 1972*


SEASONAL

I'm still growing,
expanding the limits —
my brain burgeoning
like a Georgia O'Keefe flower
dwarfing its natural landscape.

My senses boggle.
My mind flowers,
erupting in the spring's hurrah,
ebbing in the fall's amen.

The earth keeps rising to meet me,
the rain is all wrung out,
the sun's an ardent blessing,
kissing me, the weakest sprout.

*March 13- April 19, 2000*

## THE MONARCH OF DUNG

The worm emerges in a loopy dance
from its mansion of manure —
shiny under the sun,
fearful of the trowel that unearthed it.

No reveler in the loam it creates,
unpraised for beauty,
spurned as the snake for traveling on its belly
it eases out of gyration
and slides into a dark tunnel
formed by its own body.

*June 30-July 2, 1993*


## MYOPIC VIEWS

A clover is a honey bee
to the myopic eye;
a field of mustard, tiny suns
blinking in the wind.

A crow is shadow, walking
under a willow branch;
bleached wood, the chipping sparrow
beaking for a worm.

The rose is a nest for fairies;
the fence, linked paper dolls.
I, mirrored from across the room,
am just a mossy log.

Death will appear a well to me
in the thirsty drought of dying;
and my last view of verdant earth
will be water, shining.

*Dec. 12-14, 1993*

RING AROUND THE ROSY

I am given the cold shoulder of tomorrow.
The hours stalk by,
martinets as much as I
in their sixty-minute precision.

The day rides to high noon
on the impetus of timed chores.
What I wanted no longer remembered,
I brush the morning flavors
out with my broom.

The great sear of afternoon
rises from the street,
hums at my heels
its mesmerizing tones
of one two three four.

Into it I go,
the wind waltzing at my elbows,
out of time with my steps.
Flowers, sprinkled confetti,
dot the road's edges,
out of context with my mind.

Tomorrow,
the recrudescent knell resounds,
tomorrow.

*March 10-19, 1993*


REUNIONS: MARRYING WITH THE PAST

If I had nothing to measure against,
no bittersweet in retrospect,
I'd make no wearying analyses
of where I was to where I am.

I probably wouldn't think at all
just blindly nudge my way
through tasks grown heavier by the day
and know no heaven or hell.

*July 17 - 21, 2002*

## RESIDUALS: HOME SITE, ROUTE 101

Morning brought them home to me —
those two uncompromised flowering trees
that every April free of culture
blossom, graceful, on a barren site.

Long gone the house and family.
No stain on grass or ground remains,
but yet it's clear
by contour and by sheltered space
they co-existed here.

Coming up lame, limping toward night,
I gathered those blossoms to shuttered eyes;
drew up the corners of little sleep,
and buried each death I dared to dream.

*April 26-29, 2001*


## WARP-SPASM

I think of Cuchullain,
each hair of his head a spike,
a spout of black blood smoking from the skull;
Cuchullain in the weaponed chariot,
invisible under his mantle,
circling and recircling the enemy
crushing them together
in terror of the clangor and blows from the unseen
until they are all destroyed.

I think how I too have slain my thousands,
cloaking my fury in words of diplomacy,
hiding my savagery under a smile.
Over my darkness I laid my own form of disguises,
not lies but counterfeit emotions
flat as a dying face.

Yet I too have died a thousand deaths,
cowering, isolate in my fear,
pierced by what I heard and sensed,
not by what I saw.

*Nov. 3-11, 1998; June 25 - July 2, 2004*

UNEARTHING

Years ago on a fir-needled path
I followed a trail of coins —
dimes, nickels, pennies.
I gathered them all, calling aloud at each find,
"There's another one."

A month ago in drenching rain
I found a quarter two feet from the phone
where a young man conversed.
I lifted it toward him.
"Yours?"
"No," he mouthed.

Last week, I dredged one after the other
six pennies from a thawing puddle.
Two days later I found a dime close by —
the same color as winter.

Now  every day I look — anticipating, querying.
Did a drunk stumble here, sodden, uncaring,
fingering coins for keys;
a child play by this street, pretending submarines;
the earth spawn aliens in January?

At any time I may encounter,
without looking,
without expecting,
without questioning,
some intangible that
having gestated in the dark
reveals itself slowly—
like a flower to the light.

*Jan. 23-27, 2002*


PHONE CALL

How strangely my heart pleats
against the pressure of your voice! –
an accordion without music
closing in on itself,
opening again to breathe.

*1961, Summer*

## WAY STATION

They wake me, crying for breakfast.
I spread the seeds
across their tray under the window
and pray the wind won't blow,
the cat won't play sphinx
in their nests under the holly.

Miles away my mother does the same.
Only her art is different
and the need for home satisfied.
I write her:

Expect four robins before the end of March.
They spurned my feeder and chose
to arch their beaks from a snow patch
to feast on liriope berries.

They're bound by blood
to make short peace here,
an alien place for new beginnings
and the innocence of eggs in nests.

I share their reticence,
accept no terms this land can give,
and stretch my wintered limbs
toward spring and Oregon.

The feeder lies bare of birds and seeds
yet all around the strange bloods stir,
the rush of wings impatient for flight,
the air alive with unfed hungers.

*Dunwoody, Georgia*


## A TURN FOR THE WORSE

Move me into tomorrow.
Today is much too late
to honor vicissitudes of fortune
I'd rather not contemplate.

*July 26, 2000*

## UNCOMMON SENSE IN WANDERLAND

Sitting at that table set forever,
what kind of talk do you make
with a Hatter, a Hare, and a Dormouse?

A penny for your thoughts?

I have none; I'm not sitting in the right chair.
The wrong chair has no room.

Thought is naught.

You've been caught
dipping your watch in the tea.

You can't leave;
the table's unstable.
You've milk on your plate,
a tea full of crumbs,
and a worrisome trait
that nothing is something.

Neither early nor late,
time drowned in a teacup.
Face up.
Forever was yesterday.

*June 22 - July 4, 1995*

## WAKING:THE DISENGAGEMENT

There are hydras in that bosky valley
stealthy with dreams. The early morning picks
the seams of  sleep and frays it out of sequence.
The patterns I had fingered into form
are lopped off with a swipe of savagery.
Where there was one I dared to understand,
two torments rise – seductive, beckoning.

*1993*

## SIEVING

We are old lovers
but new in tastes:
not the ocean and the shore,
no; no more.

Twelve years past
divide and conquer.
Nine years past
incision.
Five years past
the iconoclast.
One year past
desertion.
Thirty days into
who-knows-what
trial or tribulation –
a mess of pottage,
the balm of Gilead,
or the usual white feather?

*Feb. 29, 1972*


## YES OR NO

She cares and she cares again
despite the wind's erupting at the eaves,
threatening the roof.
The foundation endures
built on the granite of centuries
where time makes no inroads
and no additions.
But it is not hers.

*Oct. 5 - Nov. 13, 2010*

SHUTTERED

Always this hover of rain
from November through the spring
and the salt air blossoming
on the dry buds of my tongue,
nights all on tiptoe
through the spongy lawns I knew
fully skirted with prickling fronds
soppy with unshed dew.

The unresolved rises to haunt me,
to chide my lack of courage.
Shadows become substance
and details emerge.
Everyone appears in color
with distinct shape and size,
but what I cannot resurrect
is the expression of the eyes.

*March 13-15, 2003*


THE WEB OF DARK

At night the lilac softens scent
and grief comes out of hiding.
My scars unseam and I am caught
in webs of old compliance.

Thy will, Thy will, sweet Lord, I cry,
be done, be done forever.
Loose me from the strangling lie
my dreams keep amplifying:

That death is the only reality
and hope an empty shell;
that all my losses are only one,
the stinging loss of innocence.

*1992, Late December*

# VARIATIONS ON A THEME

## JUST FOR PLAY

My mouth salt-pebbled,
I think of Demosthenes,
a voice against waves,
his intention to be heard
over the bellowing sea.

He must have learned soon
how gradations are required
when the blood is hot —
timing the waves' crescendo
through the diminuendo.

I learned his lesson,
stifling the desire to shout
at fulmination,
to voice my seasoned outrage
mellifluously.


## A SECOND FOR PLAY

Like a wraith of Demosthenes,
sluicing my words through salt,
I burble into the sea,
the waves responding
glissando (perhaps in Greek?),
leaving their scrabbled messages
a froth at my feet.

*June 18-23, 2002*

WEDDING TWO WORLDS
(To Mike)

The night is splintering in small pieces,
abstract like a shifting kaleidoscope.
All the roads are running backwards,
the street signs smeary with rain.

"You'll never find it," son Mike had said
over the phone, hopeless, trapped miles away
with a motorcycle requiring repairs.

I drove forever, passed intersection after intersection
buffeted by my brain's lack of direction.
A pause, my foot light on the accelerator,
"This feels about right." My lips formed the words
of the sign glistening in that black wet —"Steve Street."

Why hadn't I remembered?
I had been here with my son Steve,
laughingly noting the coincidence,
at this cycle shop where the owners' Doberman
answered to the same name as ours — Rommel.

Out of every darkness light comes.
Move into the space of the unknown? Revelation is unpredictable.
Steve, dead since mid-summer — back to guide me.

I took the turn, rounded the corner, pulled to the curb
Back-lit by the warm yellow light from the garage
was Mike, substantial, relieved.
I stepped out, reentering
by handing him the key.

*Jan. 14-17, 2010*

## SEPTEMBER MATTERS

Before vision clears —
a hound fetal-curled beneath a madrone,
a slug stretched atop the euonymus,
a frog sheltered in a rose.

Seeing by hope is easy:
The hound rouses shaking off sleep,
the slug munches on leathery leaves,
the frog snugs into the relaxing petals.

Vision focuses, revealing
the hound is a surface root,
the slug a dried leaf,
the frog a blob of errant green.

Vision falters.
There is no market for false impressions,
their images stamped on a receptive brain
and filed under oblivion.

*Sept. 2-7, 2008*


## WHIMSICAL NOTE

The rosebush
aware of multiple births
shows no favoritism,
aborts no buds,
knowing the environment
favors the strongest.
Determination is not
the bent of mothers.

*Sept. 2003*

## REMEMBERING PAVAROTTI

The refrigerator sings,
audible over the aria of the furnace
like the soprano over the tenor.
When neither performs,
silence raises its untrained voice —
infantile, unintelligible.
You cannot take its measure
until that is all there is.

*Sept. 11-12, 2009*


## THE SLANT

I sense your shard of heart
that leans in to me
hoping for the old succor –
as ancient only as last year.

*July 16, 1971*


## RECOGNITION

She sits now in a wheelchair
who formerly stood so tall,.
the distance between us in calendar years
no more than a breath, a decade.

A personal reading I cannot take.
I live one day at a time,
for the diurnal sweep precludes no dawn.
Tomorrow does not wait.

*April 20, 2003*

PRELUDE TO AUTUMN

A silence sits
on this greensweet morning:
the slug lifting its horned head
from the quilt of Baby's Tears,
the great wall of Escallonia
studded with pink blossoms,
the prickly scent of encroaching fall
rising from ankle-deep Sweet William.

I sink my hands
into the dry crumbling earth,
lift out a surplus of lemon mint,
rubbing the dusty leaves between my fingers,
savoring the faint aroma.

Mid-August distills the season's turn,
regret for seeds unplanted,
flowers left to run rampant,
the melody of growth strangely dissonant
in the subtle change.

The undergrowth rots,
losses multiply,
and time funnels down
into a dry watering can.

*Aug. 17-18, 1994*


PLAY-ACTING

A splintered vision haunts the brain,
twists the limbs and tickles the senses
to force them through a rough pastiche
and create form where none exists.

A being spawned by instinct's spark
can tread the boards from 8:00 to 10:00
then snuggle in its fetal sack
and gestate for another birth.

The act repeated grows in strength
from puling cries to resonance
until no artifice remains,
until the player becomes the played.

*Sept. 6-9, 2001*

READING BACKWARDS

The black letters on the white page
squirmed into words given emotional weight,
suggesting communication.
Nothing afterward was ever the same.

"I wish you could talk the way you write," he said.
Talk is cheap, I thought, not safer.

Now all those letters forming words
snug to each other in envelopes
labeled with place names  where I lived.
Time travel will come soon enough.
These older eyes will read them again,
perhaps make the same interpretations,
perhaps not.

*Jan. 21-25, 2009*


REVIVALS

Your face,
the lean jaw, the straight of brow,
is memorized;
your scent stored,
of tree bark and ferny woods,
The light-footed rolling gait,
the stealth of your steps,
the exquisite simplicity
of your long-fingered hands —
these I keep.
They waken with a startle,
a similar in someone else.

But your voice I cannot draw
from lush yesterdays,
the vibrancy, the lilting inflections
that carried a smile.
Perhaps
in this fall of the twelfth year,
in this giant stand of redwoods
where all sound is hallowed,
I may.

*Oct. 28-31, 1993*

## FACING IT

Mirror, mirror on the wall,
I'd like to shatter when you fall;
for Truth is warm as summer's song,
but lies leave death upon the tongue.

*June 8, 1971*


## REFUGE

Everyone has his silver swan
enticing with its very air.
It floats atop a placid pool
in undulating harmony.

And one can go there
when he wills, what disturbs
left far behind.
Water shimmering,
water soundless,
glinting silver, glinting light.

*Dec. 26, 2012 - Jan. 3, 2013*


## A MESS OF POTTAGE

Your muted anger
against my questioning
seels truth's bright eye.
Regretfully, August and September
lie underneath my brow.

I shatter in the frame
you place for me
and mirror gullibility
as pale and secret shame.

And here and now?
Ah, God, dear God,
I think that I've been had.

*June 8, 1971*

## NO SEEKERS, NO FINDERS

He lay on his stomach in a ditch
peering at me as I at him,
fifty years between us.

I read him and he read me,
a stand-off in a moment:
The intersecting streets were bare;
no clues were walking anywhere.

His eyes kept dancing,
daring me
to show I guessed why he was there
by reacting overtly.

No chance.
I've been under beds, in closets,
behind bushes, beneath houses,
always in the dusk or dark
until some sharp eyes probed the spot,
impaling me, and I was caught.

Betray a hiding place?
Not me.
I am in hiding myself.

*Aug. 3-9, 1995*


## OPTICAL

Your eyes probe for the nerve.
I feel them cleaning
precise as a crab,
meticulous as a beetle
stripping old bone bare.

I could hang there —
a specimen impaled —
scoured of thought,
my mind a desert wall
soaking up sun.
But I am neither an insect
nor an orange.

*Jan. 31, 1980, Dunwoody*

## ON FINDING AN EMPTY SNAIL SHELL IN JANUARY

Hey, there, Janus,
you two-faced
son of a drizzle,
pod-popper,
frond-whipper,
cannibal to rose nipples —
your rotten breath
all through the garden —
set your double endowment
of eyes on this:

The flesh is gone
but the shell is there.
Perfect,
crisp,
it lies upon the soil
spiraled
at the base of a blooming tulip.

*Jan. 24, 1993*


## ON A GRECIAN ROSE

When evening dampens, pressing close,
the names of flowers erupt in dance —
alyssum, thrift, and candy tuft,
impatiens, cosmos, and four o'clocks.
What's in a name? Each to its own.

As darkness deepens, the names disperse,
settle indiscriminate as to form,
which belonging to which a puzzle,
the references denied.

With morning light, twelve inches high
the Grecian Rose affirms itself.
Neither red nor orange but Crayola- hued,
it crinkles, a fluted cup of wrinkled smiles,
and freely sows its summer seeds
to spark the memory under next year's sun.

*May 23-30, 2008*

LIVING BY DEFAULT

Days spent in hiding,
cloaked glances sweeping over recognition,
atmosphere gauged by guess,
instinct uncertain but acted on.
Life goes astray,
out of step with the distant drummer.

Morning comes in over the blue hills,
stretches over the ocean.
The grass plastered with rain,
slippery with slugs,
offers its sweet green scent.

*May 18-22, 2005*


HALF A RENAISSANCE

So long have children bloomed upon the horizon
that, today, when you came Proteus from the sea,
in mid-afternoon, bearing a great ribboned pot of cyclamen,
I trembled joyous in my timid earth,
five years away from roots of youth and spring.

When first we were married, I could say to you easily,
naturally, in the slowness of wakings,
"How like a lush rich berry you bloom on my pillow."
Your strong masculine features would quirk and dip
at the softness of the attack.

Then when your magnificent eyes were covered
by sleep, I'd study your foreign maleness,
savor the splendor of beard surfacing
on your brown cheeks and chin,
marvel at the crisp finger curls sprouting
from your chest.
I had known no other man before you.

When the children came – one, two, three in as many years,
I lost the curve of your horizon
in the bitter after-births of turn and work
and turn and work again.

*Feb. 14, 1967*

OUTLIVING THE MYTH
(For Laura)

Once upon a time
when a slipper shaped the foot,
the girl was tamed,
became Princess-Forever-Happy
in the only acceptable dream.

Years vanished.
Then something in her tapestry of days tarnished,
the golden illusory thread.
Affirmatives disappeared, slithered
elusive as lizards from exposure.

She learned of Sylvia,
hunched at the oven
inhaling sweet gas;
and Marge squirreling
in the secrecy of drink;
of Iris forever sifting ashes
seeking one live coal.

She closed it off beneath her lids,
nightly wandering through fields of sun,
catching clover around her ankles,
pebbles in her socks.
Then she banished from her kingdom
all calendars and clocks.

*Oct. 2-17, 1995*


A SNAPSHOT OF VENOM

Wed to woes she was,
as splintery as fresh-sawed wood.
You didn't want to be around her —
that dark miasma seeping into you.

She pins you with those close-set eyes,
drowning you with the stale sludge
of past grievances pouring from her mouth.
Everything in you retracts, the day muddied.

*March 2 – April 3, 2009*

122

MAGIC ACTS

Look.
Gossamer scarves knotted end to end
blurring colors, spilling from my sleeve,
and here a rabbit with surprised ears
popping from my hat.

What do you think?

Can I share
with words that fashion substance from air,
open doors to let light in,
and even in the dark of pain
ignite the sky with a cloud-spawned moon?

If you cannot answer yes,
there is no less a magic force
for me who can slake a haunting thirst
by tilting last year's tulip cup
and swallowing spring in a single gulp.

*May 18 - June 1, 1997*


MIDNIGHT INDULGENCE

Sometimes I am defined by these yellow walls,
one with a closet, two with windows, one with a door.
On the nights the moon burns so fiercely through the pines
that it wakes me, I half-rise,
study the artificial stars placed on the ceiling years ago.
It is always newly strange.
Possibilities lie in all directions.

The closet is full of years,
time spent trailing behind me.
The windows offer scent and muted sound,
time static having no measure.
The door extends its invitation
to close, to open, to leave by.

*March 24-30, 2008*

## ON INTRODUCING A LACE-CAPPED HYDRANGEA

I drew up the earth like a blanket,
a soft sigh over my hands,
tucking in the hydrangea
with its lacy blossom facing the sky —
blue stars on a snowy crown.

(I am a child breathing against a frosted window,
the dark deepening in the center of white,
the pattern flowering out in whorls from the warmth.)

The sky is falling in summer rain.
Salt, it lies on my lips surprising me.
The air flutters full of wet sounds
punctured by the crows' dark caws.

Someone has dropped bread on the waters.
The hunger beneath the surface is fed.

*July 28-29, 1997*


## GROUNDED

I lost a coin purse
the color of old brick,
no bigger than my hand.
How neatly it fit there
holding only a library card,
names of authors whose books I enjoyed,
and the simplest of identification.

The next day I retraced my route—
around the park, through the woods,
past the Blue Star memorial
and to my resting bench
cornered across from the sleeping trees.
There it sat in the grass,
soft and fresh with rain,
just where I tuck my feet.

*Feb. 27 - Mar 3, 2007*

## IMPENDING

It lurks in the twigged shade chanting dirges
to thrum in the head of the listener
just beyond the door of night
in the plucking wind of December.

The petals of fall have long gone brown.
The crows have coarsened their cawing.
The carols of frost-spun winter sift
through the bare-boned limbs of the laurel.
The closet of morning stands open to lies
the mirror has dusted over;
the welcoming pillow comforts last year's dreams
in the sting of the salt sea air.

Go steady, old one, frame yesterday now
in the mauve of the sunset you knew
lest the beast in the shadows fade to a wraith
and insinuate itself into you.

*Dec. 5-7, 1993; Dec. 12, 2005*


## CLOSED CIRCLE

The curve of fraud
is wide indeed.
It rounds one in, completes itself
and shuts the other person out.

The quickest knife,
the sharpest sword
has lesser power
than the word.

For love is strung
like a marionette
controlled by mind and hands;
and if the tongue sits
tight and dark,
deceit has power over the heart.

*March 9, 1972*

ILLUSION, ILLUSION
(For Melissa)

They come back
with their secret faces,
an accommodation to the dark
and silent spaces of their identities,
their words sweet pulp on the tongue.

Fragments all of them
that whisper from the shadows of the stage:
You have played us
so that you might dream our dreams
fashioned from the uncharted dark of words
and set like prisms on the horizon,
affirming that life reveals
facet by facet
only as it reflects light.

*Sept. 4-8, 1993*


WHOSE LITTLE CYCLAMEN ARE YOU?

In mossy mealy hands I hold you rare,
composite of bold green and crimson hearts.
I plant you in the richest cache of earth,
for your crazy rage of blossom shakes the spring.

You nuzzle, start, and whiffle down my battens,
you double-hearted son of a sylvan sprite.
I plant you like a body under noon time,
for your little tease of blossom whispers spring.

It's long past youth and spring has summered.
Each year breaks more blossoms down to earth.
But, I can't wing like the bird of prey
with the strange hungry beak of yesterday.

I'm earthbound, narrowed by culture,
downed from the dazzle of soar. I am snugged like a bulb
in the shade of love; and given time to grow
in the moss, the mold, and the charcoal, under a sky of shine.

*Feb. 20, 1967*

THE GREEN EYE

My gazanias extend in down,
cottoning the earth.
Greedily I dust
their silent wings,
thwarting the robber wind
who'd lavishly flower
my vacant-eyed neighbor
instead of me.

I dare to move
against the drift of blossom,
the daft benevolence of growth;
close down May
in orange shallows
and barbarously slap
this mulch on magic,
incontinence the wind.

No native flower
will sprout in foreign womb.
No fickle flight
of seed will bloom,
and, talon-sharp, flash
fiesta-red to bull
my rage at flippant chance.

I cannot trust a profligate
to honor my selection,
contrarily choose a wind, my seeds,
to regenerate each season.

*1970's, La Mesa*


A REFUSAL

You bring me your night.
I cannot harbor there
in your great sea of compassion.
I am afraid of the dark.

*July 13, 1993*

# A SERIES OF IMPRESSIONS WHEN PLUMS ARE PRUNES

## NOVEMBER

The cloud-raddled moon
nurses no stars,
slips points of light through the firs.
The night holds earth in its chilly arms
and the dew keeps falling.

## FULL CIRCLE

First, there is a room,
then a  hall, a house,
a fence, a street.
Last, the order reverses.

## PUZZLES

Jigsaws and crosswords
require similar talents —
a memory for connections,
a modicum of reason.

## SIMILARITY

The bark on the tree
has nothing on me.
I'm covered the same.
Nor do I bite.

## ANOTHER SIMILARITY

Under the skin
green as avocado,
I'm more puree
than I am solid.

*Nov. 2004*

ARTIFICIAL HORIZON
(First Flight in a Cessna 172)

Up we pitch,
frail, at strange cants,
stomachs swinging like pendulums
in a Santa Ana.

I mouth acceptables
and clutch my own
old tested talisman:
If there's an error, you only die.
The brain too tight inside its cage;
these moral wits extinguished.

Solo now?
Here in this blue-and-white skinned Cessna?
My turn to skirt around the mortal edge,
scar-stud the dazzling ceiling,
close down the horizon?

No, not here
where protesting thought descends like flaps;
not here at your discretion.

For, perhaps in this rare high shine
above the scent and pulse of earth
my absolution soars on timid wings.

Some spark struck off from deity
may light my brain,
may fire my eyes;
may stake my claim to Paradise
a generation early.

*July 18-26, 1972*

## A PARADISE OF WORDS

If I ask a little pardon,
will you let me have my sleep?
There are words that I could fashion
into sentences like fruit
that sparks a riot in the nostrils,
shapes the hands in tactile curves,
tickles all the taste buds,
and slips, voluptuous, down the throat.
If this should feed your vanity
like Omar's wine and bread,
I'll leave you in your wilderness
and go straight to my bed.

*Aug. 25-26, 2007*


## THE BILKING

I do not like you
not because I wear the spawn
of your drunkenness in my belly
but because the sight of it repels you.
How slowly breaks the bubble of illusion.
How unmanly are you, stripped indecent,
waving such a banner:
"Appearance is all!"
Obviously "in sickness and in health"
does not mean in pregnancy.

*June 5, 1972*


## HAVENS

A haven is a window garden,
a shelf of plum preserves,
the space beneath the flowering rose,
the gap between the chores.

When the day has ended
and lights erase the stars,
it's knee-deep in the shadows
the farthest from the door.

*Feb. 18, 1994*

# THE FALL OF THE YEAR

Give me the eye I'm accustomed to
that sees black in prevailing blue,
over the rainbow the advancing gray,
roses bleached on a sodden branch;

but also the moon on a starless night
needling its way through the heavy firs,
lighting the rocks that line the path,
making rhinestones of the rain.

Then give me the autumns of the past,
the blurring colors of deciduous trees
washing my eyes of dusty time,
drawing them innocent up to the hills.

*Nov. 25 - Dec. 9, 2006*


# AT THE CAUTION LIGHT

Each morning
I reacquaint with living,
threading my fingers
through the rosemary
(that's for remembrance),
moving on to the lavender,
the scent for tomorrows.

The moon pales into sky,
an easy act to follow.
I do not linger.

Blue quickens
above the weeping cedar,
its gently curved branches
sustaining a fragile green
entirely dependent
on the strength of the trunk.

*Aug. 15-29, 2011*

DISPLACEMENT

The waterdog—
dropped from a warm puppy mouth
onto the tile floor,
scooped into a dust pan,
slipped outside the gate —
how does he orient himself?

Is it a where-am-I sequence,
or does he simply
accept his startled body
and scuttle into the nearest dark?

*May 14-15, 2004*


ENIGMA

How now, brown cow,
am I to assimilate
your eternal browsing
in my back yard?

*Aug. 2004*


INTRODUCTION

This man with the scarred neck
fathers my child.
The blood of our beginning
becomes timeless:
      He covered me with himself
      so that space did not buckle in confusion.
      Bones remember the unlearned pain,
      like green optics between the eye
      and the universe.

*Oct. 23, 1961*

DELINEATION

Frost sets seams in the holly leaves
etching the integral parts.
A bit of freeze can make a point;
a thaw enhances.

*Dec. 10, 2006 – Feb. 25, 2007*


BURYING THE SUN

I dug out dandelions this morning,
all the little suns at their high noon,
and thrust them in the garbage can,
into the dark of refuse.

They glowed,
making egg shells luminous,
highlighting wet coffee grounds,
their nature baffled by the loss of joy,
buried at fruition, never to puff out
skimming over the ground on seeded threads
to the softest of touch-downs,
to sweet resurrection from a pocket of earth.

*Feb. 20 - March 2, 1995*


CONTRASTING RAGES

Inside
the air is charged —
sunlight- fixed,
my heart stiffened
my blood turgid,
the house so swollen
I cannot draw a breath.

Outside
in my garden
the rage of flowers
embraces me.

*May 6-7, 2001*

BETRAYAL

The shadow of the wind cuts,
the cold of the moon burns,
each star pierces,
breath shocks.

(Forty-one years ago
it was the same.)

*Mar 30, 2012*


FOR ERNIE'S BABY

While you sleep
the fresh coral of dawn
sweeps across the sky
emptying the pockets of dark.
Trees, houses and streets
resume form and substance.
The puddles' murky lenses
blue in the light.

When you wake
you seek only the warmth
of the arms that hold you—
with no fear of splintering sound,
no fear of falling.

*Jan. 2, 2009*


ABSORPTION

These lies
between us like unborn children
swell and startle,
sting the flesh,
and scuttle undeveloped
under summer sun.

*July 1971*

BUDDING

She came a sudden heather
of coincidence in spring, to share
with us seven cities, two countries,
and nine years.

Now Medusa in her rag-curled hair,
she startles us with slumbering promise
of blooming hips
and evident pursed breasts.

Our daughter rouses,
stirring roots of old hopes.
Uninhibited, slothful,
she caresses us, clambering astride
our knees and shoulders indiscriminately.
Her eyes, candled fires,
move us, tardily conscious
of sudden growth, childhood's demise.

She sleeps yet; but, chanticleer, tries
her voice against the waking hours;
and lays her dazzling shine
at other doors than ours. May Day!
May Day!  Whose basket of flowers?

Our baby wench
gone soft with promise
flush with spring
has pocked our time of afternoon
and wrenched us out of innocence.

*Circa 1971, La Mesa*

## FATHER READS TO THE CHILDREN

You have been mellifluous with reason,
your out-of-season smile coming and going
on the selected word "ass" in "The Musicians of Bremen."
Your children giggled each time you prefaced the word;
but, baffled by no comment, they scoured each others' faces
for transmittal of intent.

Your words rode on their attention
and lack of it:
"Who's listening?"

Back they bounded from their dessert portions.
"I am."

On you went, your eyebrows flicking,
your eyes sliding slowly at me to the right
then back again to the book.

Enchantment laced that nine-minute span;
for, dessert bowls spooned clean,
the children hovered bee-fashion,
jiggling their limbs just out of scent.
But your moment was gone —
spent —
just before adolescence.

*1975, La Mesa*


## THE WARY

Love,
in this great vortex
where I do not know
you nor you know me,
we circle warily
like suspicious foxes, scarce
daring to brush against
each other lest fur rise
primitively and raw-red
we swive the flesh from beneath.

*Aug. 17, 1971*

FOR ENIGMATIC ANN C.

A day after surgery feeling like one long scratch,
I drifted into a morphine-induced sleep.
You came in, setting down a huge tote bag
bristling with loose manuscript.

"These are for you," you said.

Then, seated, you slid your arms out on the table,
dropped your face down onto your hands,
and with your mischievous laughter filling the dark spaces
added the three words,

"And this catalog."

How like you to leave me with a conundrum,
I who struggled to make sense of your wrenched syntax,
often remaining trapped in the sticky web you spun.

How like you to leave with a laugh and no answers.

*Oct. 29-30, 2005*


JULY 1971

Proud the hoodwink!
loud the joy!
All vinegary
you pour through the house,
spilling your elation
across the stretch of tired night
holding the rest of us.

The newborn and I, freshly asleep,
feel your drunken benediction,
hand-brushed between our faces,
puerile.

*July 1971*

BLOOD TO BLOOD
(To Steve)

He was gone three nights. Spring held at bay.
She played her role of wash and serve
while the hours webbed out, laced each to each
exact as fingerprints.

The faint latch click early the third morning
stung her alert. She heard his closet step,
the creak of floor, the stealthy squish of air,
and ceased to lie immobile there with listening.

Deft in dark from years of prowling children's rooms,
she found the stairs through instinct, craft, and need.
The silence ticked; the house a brooding hen.
He wasn't there.

Her eyes appraised, her senses tested each —
the hall, the outside door, the other room.
A long thin body in an old plaid coat?
Underneath the table.

She knelt, stretched to lie full-length beside him.

"Where you been?"

"Around."

The strange brown smell of adolescence stirred
like wet leaves, worn shoes, rain-thrashed marigolds.
Light sifted through the curtains, seized the walls,
unleashed the yammering spring.

She'd never know what he had done
or where he'd been or ever forget the crooked grin
he gave her where she lay,
his mom, under the pool table
at two-thirty in the morning.

*Feb. 21, 1980*

## CHOICE OF WEAPON

I think I could dream of roses
if summer weren't so late this year —
the thick petals, each cupping each
to form their unique roundness,
and the calla lilies' fluted goblets
white as sun-bleached sheets,
erect, centered in their elephant-ear leaves.

I could dream of the moon,
tardy so many nights in keeping its promise,
easing slowly from under its cloudy quilt,
easing back into its cloudy bed.

Or I could dream past this tenuous life
accepting the invitation,
dare to slip into the field of final sleep,
dandelions brandished in my fist.

*June 22-25, 2009*

## A PAUCITY OF WIT

I won't tell you about the magpies,
how they tormented the cat
that climbed the wall by their trees.
You wouldn't accept that birds could be evil.

If I disguised them,
told you they were the blackest of witches
with noses steely and sharp as switch-blades,
that their wings were cloaks
walloping like muted thunder
in the plunge to their prey,
you might listen, your mouth agape.

But if you want a bedtime story,
I could hide the remembered horror
in metaphor and cliché.

*March 5-8, 2008*

## HAIKU SERIES

Reverberations
from the small hail, crisp drumbeats
ushering out March.


Spring sun startles me,
rupturing the play of clouds.
Winter holds its breath.


The blaze of spring sun
burns my eyelids. I weaken
purged by the onslaught.


Crows telegraph spring
from tree to tree, raucous claims
against the squirrels.


Gray rain from blue skies
silences the cheep of birds
in their April nests.

*April 4-6, 2003*



## A SLAP IN THE FACE

Some young girl with her butternut flesh
her whip-quick thighs and her depthless eyes
lies;
and lies;
and lies on the half-shell of my husband's heart.
The bitter days rain down their residue
where art has no study
nor child its father
nor womb its due.

How careless is the pledge of troth –
words that bind the mind but not the flesh,
taken like promises offered on cue,
given like gifts to guile a wife.
          Hurt is all of yesterday and half of life.

*Feb. 24, 1972*

140

IN PERPETUITY

I left love
in a black box of a house
in suburban Atlanta.

The new owners welcomed its alien warmth,
put it on with their clothes,
served it for breakfast.

When they wearied of it,
it wandered spectral, unclaimed,
haunting their days and nights.

They sold the house, moved out.
It stayed, an undeclared resident.

*Aug. 9-15, 2006*


LAMENT OF THE SIXTIES

Half-past forty is a sounding of years.
The mind churns a babble of noise.
The tongue lies mute behind the smile
and the eyes speak words.

The world pieces and unpieces
as reflections in open water
displaced by a sudden movement
turn again to image.

The mind stands still,
nudges blindly through a maze,
finds an exit curiously
and stumbles on the phrase it sought;
but the lips don't fit the words
and tangled is the speech,
hesitant, apologetic,
and quaintly released.

*Nov. 25-27, 1993*

HEDGES
(For Larry)

You asked about hedges
against the wind,
salt air,
and blowing dust.
I described their pattern.
They widen as they lengthen,
become impenetrable
(except for cats and sparrows)
enclosing the wild iris and Montebretia
until at last they become a wall
that only a bitter freeze can soften,
nipping off leaves,
letting in light.

I did not say
hedges are barriers against despair,
cloisters for the heart frosted
long before the body winters;
that they shelter snakes, slugs, and ant castles
all a-jumble;
and if you weed,
you rake out last year's leavings
moist with memory.

No, I told you
only what you asked.

*Jan. 16-20, 1994*


EXPOSED

Inland, waiting out the storm,
the gulls forage,
paddling through the soppy grass,
see-sawing from tail to ravenous beak,
bobbling  with the wind
in their foreign sea:

> A quirky majesty in how they float,
> alien to the field, their slickly white bodies
> stark against the green,
> flocked, sheltered
> out in the open.

*March 20 – April 1, 2012*

ECHOES

In dreams the past returns
patchworked with sense,
stitched with nonsense,
but no comprehensible nuance.

> I emerged from the building
> with a present-day habit,
> a half cigarette in a case,
> and a lighter that failed.
> You in a white suit
> (you never owned one)
> strode up offering a matchbook,
> something you hadn't carried for thirty years.
> We strolled along
> cigarette smoke curling around your head
> (a habit you dropped fifteen years ago).

We were young, unburdened with time,
moving easily and naturally
through a dream fragile as breath.

*Feb. 1-4, 2009*


HANDING OVER
( To Laurie)

This hard walk into the socking wind,
the brown dust of summer peppering me
proves me leaning into winter,
compressing autumn into hours under my feet.

My sun melts down into your tomorrow,
leeching light from paths we shared,
trails through the wilderness, hand-in-hand.

I relinquish my hold,
passing it like a talisman
to you and the grandchild
moving toward uncharted hills and valleys.

Only the high plains lie before me,
the eye measuring the distance to the horizon.
Behind me, the forest has closed in.

*Sept. 12-21, 1994*

THE HYGIENIST

In the long nights I dream
of teeth cozy in their pink saucers,
of their dark dome-ridged cavern
where my gloved fingers
wield picks and scrapers and brushes,
wary of the tongue flicking side to side.

On those nights when uppers and lowers
do the natural thing—
bite down on what's between them,
masticating and savoring —
I wake grappling with reality,
scrabbling with my bloody stumps.

*Nov. 13-16, 2008*


IN ABEYANCE

Morning sleeps in the rosebuds
sealed with dew.
Expectation thumbs at the crossroads
seeking an exit.
Time keeps in that watch
placed somewhere back of yesterday
for the sixth move in seven years.

But, an unnamed something trembles forever
in a bubble of sleep
burst by the floor-mopper's soapy fingers
pinching my eyelid open
to see if I were dead.

*July 17-22, 2001*


POST-PARTURITION

I cradle my newborn in the hourless time
and sense her father's jubilation like soft burrs,
thrust upon the wind.

How blurred those days, how gross the passions:
Me with my newborn; he with his.

*Feb. 24, 1972*

BARRED

Minou, a pale yellow parakeet,
house guest for six weeks,
has gone silent,
staring the hours away
before a cracked mirror.

I differ little,
looking backward,
finding a similar distortion;
the half-century wavering
in and out of light,
a curious mismatch of reflections;
my world no more than a cage
from which in one thin moment
I may slip
and, clipped for eternity,
fall into dust.

*April 19-20, 1995*


THE COLOR OF LABOR

The escallonia squeezes out little trumpets.
Rhododendrons hold their promises
rigid before unfolding.
Even the humble peacock orchid
writhes in its petals.
Some buds take days to open;
others harden or turn to mush.
Varied colors shriek at bloom
revealing more or less an effort
by their hue.

If beauty is produced from pain,
then maybe from my hard-earned dust
red roses will erupt.

*April 29 - May 4, 2003*

CROSSING PATHS

In his special place out of the wind,
he sat in his wheelchair, one leg missing,
the other footed on the ground.

Often we chatted. He had a wife
and an ex-wife living nearby.
Not much was personal.

One day he had a companion, a baby gull,
that strayed no farther than six inches from him.
"Don't know," he said. "It just showed up."

He was always there, happily observant
of everything — vehicles with waving drivers,
pedestrians, park workers, the weather.

The last time I saw him he said
he had been in and out of the hospital.
I nodded, acknowledging his frailty.

Weeks passed, moving from summer to fall.
Only dry leaves rattle on his strip of concrete.
I never knew his name.

*Dec. 8-10, 2009*


INCUBUS

All my dreams are water dreams
of brown bear rivers that hug my knees
and draw me slowly under.
With eyes fright-shut I gape
in cruel agony like the starved
neglected Angel in the aquarium.

Bright-eyed, clashing soundless,
I thunder only in my throat.
When expiration flashes in my skull,
I writhe my legs gone mermaid
and gulp the slug of breath
that bursts my heart.

*April 1974*

## GOODBYE ON A GENTLE AFTERNOON

I am bereft though bereft is a nothing,
like the phantom sense of an amputated limb,
the useless muscles of an empty womb,
like the heart beat mimicking a suddenly silenced drum,
the reverberation following the pipe organ's thrum,
the wail long-gone of a departing train,
and the night ear listening for the hiss of rain.

*May 31 - June 9, 2002*


## INEVITABLY

July is the sad month," she said.

The light dispersed.
The night flowed in
to pool behind the curtains.

In the morning it would be August.

*Sept. 14-16, 2012*


## TURNAROUND

You unpredictable November—
the wind astonished,
the rain dissolved in puddles,
the crows purple-blue,
the sky scared white —
how are you bringing
the scent of May?

*Nov. 19 - Dec. 2, 2012*

MORNING SUNSHINE
(For Jeannette and Rachael)

Into the thin morning they came,
two little girls.
Polite,
they clattered quietly
and tucked in their smiles,
roses ready to bloom.

They savored the French toast I made,
one eating with a  fork,
the other with her fingers;
then swiped the napkins
across their bud mouths.
"Did you have enough?"

"Yes, I'm full," the younger answered,
"but I'd really like to lick the plate."

"Go ahead," I said, turning away.
"I won't look."

"No," she decided solemnly.
"I don't think I will."

Later I found hairbrushes.
"You don't want to look like slobs."

The older,
a flash of white teeth
too large for her mouth,
lover of big words,
giggled at the coarse one.

Then they were gone
and all my other mornings of children —
small sisters and brother,
my own four —
gathered in the lap of sunshine
flooding the empty chairs.

*Aug. 9 - Oct. 12, 1998*

## LORDS OF THE SUBWAYS

These late March worms silent in their sludge,
last year's decaying grass, thick, black,
steamy as manure, rouse at the trowel's entrance,
spin, coil, or lie turgid stunned by the sun.

Their dark warm beds compost through winter,
quilt-thick, studded with pill bugs.
Small things, uncovered, helpless,
they startle and wink at the light.

I lift whole dormitories of them,
writhing and curling like strands of marcelled hair.
Transplanted, their lush murky passageways
enlarge the mulberry's bole for flower beds.

Seeds and bulbs gone to earth last fall
thrust green horns upward through the loosening soil;
feel the spring warm at their cores,
the silky promise of worms swimming in their roots.

*March 1980*


## MUSIC OFF THE SPHERE

The moon unquiet at 3 A.M.
burned music in my head.
The night in the corners began to thrum
and a chorus responded beneath the bed.

I did not willfully choose the hour
to orchestrate the impending day,
but all of tomorrow began to flower
before I had put today away.

Strange how closely I monitored hours
when sleep lay far beyond my reach.
A little night music sprouted flowers
and the dawn flared up, a torch.

*Oct. 1, 1996*

## THE MORNING OF THE WHITE BALLOONS

It tapped me on the shoulder, a white balloon.
I could have taken its dangling string
and tethered myself to rise above the earth,
subject to whatever current flowed.
But, I let it pass over into the pine grove.

Another touched down just ahead of me,
its smooth cheek abrading against asphalt.
It bounced, lifted, accepting the wind's pull,
and angled left toward the river.

I, the plodder, too solid for the wind,
must dream and await on leaden feet
my time to loft, to soar.

*June 24 - July 15, 2007*


## LADY-IN-WAITING

I track you in the pale reaches of dawn
and the winged swirls of night.
I will find you when you least expect me.

The promise ages, as a stunning bruise
not evident when first received
darkens and extends.

Days come up and days go down,
alternate sides of the same known face.

In the holding bed
death hides its smile in the blankets.
The sky crackles like paper
around the new moon invisible in the old.

Under the morning door
the sun slides a secret message.

*Dec. 1-5, 2004*

## MID-AUGUST

The pulse of summer is thready,
the sift of fall rustling
before its turn;
the shade deepening,
shaping itself toward night.

The wind offers dust
to constrain me
in the same dry pocket
where growth is confined to memory
and only the mind reaches
reaches
to startle the hardened senses.

*Aug. 13-18, 1998*


## LIVING ON AIR

The Dachshund twitches its nose
testing morning by scent,
its tail readied
for what circumstance requires,
up, down, wig-wag.

The human, less certain,
darts his eyes left, right, straight ahead,
listens almost unconsciously.

Each puffs breath,
silvery as moonlight
and as insubstantial.
Each searches for intrusion.

The Dachshund noses the yard,
suspicious corners twice,
barking to announce his territory inviolate.
The human gleans for the words
for the white butterflies sucking up nectar,
for the hummingbirds whirring over the fuchsia —
impatient for impressions to flow
through his blood,
into the pen,
onto the redemptive paper.

*Aug. 16-22, 2009*

MASKS

SCRAP I

I was born with a veil on my face.
According to folklore, that was a sign
of good luck and second sight;
but since neither ever afflicted me,
I discounted it soon enough.
I am inclined, however, to think
that is why I see darkly.

SCRAP II

It began with Eve, tasting the forbidden fruit.
Ashamed, she had to hide from what she knew.
All disguises were born there
from leaves and vines to underwear
and excuses, excuses, excuses.

"We were cold," she said.
Justifying the wrong might make it right.
But, had she not broken the terms of the lease,
awakening herself to a denial of rights,
we'd all be there now
with no need for lawyers.

SCRAP III

It is marketing yourself over and over
covering your inadequacies
that becomes tiresome.
Without that subterfuge,
you are vulnerable.
I've had enough of that too.

*July 23-28, 2002*

## WHISTLING IN THE DARK

The wind
exhaling witch cries
stirs the old wood pile,
tumbling pill  bugs on their backs,
alerting the slugs' antennae;
rousing all the spooks
from their subterranean haunts
to perform with throaty hums
their high-wire tricks,
hanging by a toe, a finger, or an elbow.
Faces malleable as rubber
squint and leer, turn upside-down
or sideward; stretch their lips
to expose pickety teeth
and tongues thick and rounded
like colored cookie-dough rolls.
With a rustle, sweep, and swoosh
the full band scratches at the house foundation
and scrabbles up the siding.

Night is pasted on the window.
They can't get in.


## MAC 6500 (INTRODUCTION TO)

In this alien field
I am looking
for the universal arrow.
I must guide by instinct
or perhaps hope
before the unraveling begins,
before thought disappears into stupor
and whatever vision was possible
is erased by a darkened screen.

*June 1998*

MOVEMENTS

The rotting log is a hall
where slugs cavort
antenna to retracted antenna
in a slurpy dance,
issue out for their morning aerobics
snacking on the yellow-green
of the euonymus
before the sun rises.

I loft them with a trowel
to the farthest corner
of the yard.

What must it be
to travel as if winged
for one glorious second,
drop to soft grass,
woozy, motion-sick,
uncurl one's self
and inch dew-dazzled home.

*May 19-23, 2004*


MAY 1971

Now that I'm no longer yours,
you offer me yourself – in bits
and pieces – no good for solace;
and think the same old use
of casual counters will suffice
for wife. Ah, no, the bonnet
is alive with bees and more than
"Thank you, Love" and "If you please"
required.

Mark this, Dearest,
mark it well:
I love you only
half the hell's
worth you've given.

*May 18, 1971*

LIMERICK

There was a young man named Burpee.
"The worst name in the world!" cried he.
"With two fores and no aft,
I've gone a bit daft,
so lettuce turnip and pea."

*Dec. 2000*


OF BABY BEN, VINTAGE 1941

"It'll still run if you turn
it upside down."

Darn it, son,
that clock is older
than you are.
It's thirty-three
on Christmas
and its face
is as familiar
as my own.
I cannot read it
when it's not
as it ought
to be, set
snug to tick
against the nights.

Its time still keeps
for me. I'll try
it on its side
—it's running now —
and hope somehow
you'll understand
that what I've loved
for years and years
is not to be subjected
to a complete reversal
like standing it
on its head.

*Dec. 12, 1974*

THE MIRRORED PAST

On a half-stripped branch of the shore pine
three mourning doves converged.
Odd how they merely suggested reality,
like the static figures in a medieval painting.
Or was it that the stillness in their communion
so transferred I could not seat myself
in my human world ?

One whooshed purposefully away
leaving the two desultory, indecisive
whether to stay and peck on the leavings
or wing away on their own.

How many little quivers,
how many little surrenders
before the mirror cracks?

*Aug. 17-20, 2012*


OFF WITH THE OLD

Again, the backward journey,
uncharted,
is paragraphs of prose
and ageless photographs
taken by the senses
decades ago.

The New Year looms monumental:
365 giant steps.
May I?
Yes, you may.

It's only permission to move:
an invitation to a puppet's party
where nightmare pulls the strings
for an audience as empty
as the stage is full.

*Dec. 27, 1992*

## LETTING IT GO

How stilled life is
on this promontory
absent the you and me
vibrant with youth.

Today, a gray morning,
water and sky inseparable,
I refuse to seek a horizon,
to reach for what is lost.
There is a warm yellow
blooming only a few steps
from where I stand.

*July 28-30, 2010*


## THE MAGIC PILLOW

December magic quiet as snow
comes at night, drifts through the pillow
in feathery whispers that lure me, baseless
to forgotten rooms with remembered faces.

Like Scrooge on his journey through Christmas Past,
I take up emotions and hold them fast;
but carry along the years since then
that color the picture, revive each sin.

There is always strangely the sense of haste,
the threat of expulsion, the fall from grace
back to an earth grown cold with age
and always before me the printed page

of what's to come: the failing sense,
the thundering guilt, the recompense
for wasted time and numbing fears
that kept me silent through the years.

It's my puff of fancy, my pinch of shame
that the old year turns upon a dream
that sieves the past to find the treasures;
then raises a new year from the ashes.

*Jan. 1-12, 1995*

## OF BRUNNEHILDE, NEWLY WELPED

Nights glut my consciousness
with all I fear to feel.
Sleep is what I know awake;
dawn is tied around my feet.
Yet Death is walking through the house —
natural, perpetuating.

Death is silky, long of limb,
arrow-swift in flight.
Death is black with four huge paws
and eyes like safflower oil.

Death is a matron with trailing pups
that fight to suckle her.
God protect me from the thought:
Death feeds her progeny.

*Circa 1973*


## SILLY WILLIES

A ghost is a disembodied body.
How can you say it is real?
It comes from nothing,
unbidden,
creates not even a flutter in the air,
leaves
without disturbing anything.

Is it real because you see it?
Mirages fade as you come nearer.
Does it slip through a crack in the mind
or from  a crack in another world?

Only on the wrong side of time
will you know.
Now there is only
the ghost of an idea,
the ghost of a smile,
the ghost of your former self.

*Sept. 29 - Oct. 7, 1998*

# PROMISES, PROMISES

Promises
in the barest rim of the moon
growing slowly out of the mountain
and, in its fully formed body,
at 2 A.M. sliding in the window
and stretching out on the bed.

Promises
in children's eyes,
they who carry no burden of prophecy
or consciousness of fleeting time.

Promises
in the remembered words of my aunt,
"I want to live just long enough
to welcome the new century."

Promises
of new years come and gone
to us who know Buck Rogers and "1984";
who know that 2000 may speak
of greener fields and richer years
offering more than promises.

*Dec. 10, 1997*


# COMING HOME

He told me:

I could hear running feet
and a woman calling,
"I don't usually chase after young men,
but you've got to stop!"

I turned, thinking maybe I'd dropped something.
I had, but it was an impression.

"Oh," she said, her eyes milky blue with tears,
"You look just like your father."

I moved on in that bubble of warmth for hours.
My dad died when I was eleven months old.

*June 26, 1993*

ON WINGS OF FIRE
(In Praise of Bandon)

I was the city asleep.
Buried in ashes twice,
I thrust up to exist
not to thrive.
Fed by legend,
I seemed to lie fallow
in my rich stand of gorse
awaiting the final fire.

Did you catch my act?
Out of the dark —
my shroud, my tomb —
I loosed into light
squat and stumpy,
absurd as a creature of flight.
Did you watch me bumbling,
fat and creeping,
pumping up my wings
to drink the sun,
forget the womb —
the long night shrunk
to a wrinkle?

See? I fly!
How quick the eye
to catch the flash of flight
but miss the subtlety of growth
from chrysalid to wings.
I loft, I light,
I glory in the flower.
Transformed,
I am embodied fire,
the rainbow promise given wings.

*Oct. 1983-1984*

INTOXICATION

I must read T.S. Eliot again.
I've not read Eliot since - when?

Under doors and around windows
blows the breath of other days
foul with rot and sweaty clothes,
the scrabbled body the dog unearthed.

To and fro he followed his nose
through graying wieners, remnants of buns,
greasy papers, and spongy fries.
No difference to him to gnaw from the bones
the bloodied meat of a human face.

*April 1-7, 2004*


TRANSLATION

I came home
to June's rampant sea
of undulating grass,
the overgrown green
hiding the dead.

Above, orange and yellow calendulas
hawked their beauty;
the clove pinks stretched
for open earth.
I pulled.
Great clumps stripped loose
scattering slugs,
baring a swath of rich loam,
a cache,
an inheritance
won by the simplest of exertions,
a tug at the roots.

*June 27-30, 1994*

A SIMPLE QUIRK

Once I took a lover,
imaginary,
for my left brain,
to serve as a rudder;
blind as I was,
shapeless as tomorrow
in a ninety-six-degree house
fueled by the L.A. sun.

I was insular,
fanning the fires of the senses,
amok in that miasmic air,
except for him.
He was always there
circling,
nudging me
toward the proper sphere.
Now years away
at sixty degrees,
fresh fevers burn
in the quivering senses,
the swirl and welter of advancing years.
But imagination is bereft
on the barren coast,
the left brain rudderless,
dormant,
adrift.

*Aug. 22-31, 1994*


SEASONING

Stillborn
this morning —
no scent of the sea,
no rupture of crows
winging and squawking—
an October quirk,
the introduction to dormancy,
the sun sifting auburn
on the grasses,
amber on the weeds.

Tomorrow will be south wind
and rain spattering,
south wind and rain,
the excruciatingly
beautiful wrench
to the season.

*Oct. 12-25, 2012*


THE OUTSKIRTS OF EDEN

Night, cropped to fit around the shrubs
and lie in the depths of the trees.
Light, cupped to rain on the streets
away from the wooden fence
where the young man hoped himself invisible.

"Are you all right?"
I asked before I read the air around him,
recalled he was a newly-wed.

"Yeah," he said.

I walked on,
carrying his misery as my own,
the first shattering of the bliss of marriage;
remembered the shock,
the useless attempt to gather the pieces
— and mending — mending with scars.

*Sept. 2-6, 2002*


TELLING TIME

How carefully the time goes by,
start and stop by the second hand.
Clocks watch movement guardedly,
but watches clock the essence.

*April 5-6, 2006*

## DINING OUT

What's on the menu today?

Cedar tips garlanded with rain,
dark domes of mushrooms,
shreds of red pine needles,
savory salt air —
all the usuals.

And the specials?

Everything unseen but felt,
registered but silent:
Actions regretted but not atoned for,
laughter restrained for fear of censure,
sympathy withheld for self-preservation.

Are you ready to order?

Give me a little more time.

*Nov. 20-22, 2009*


## INTO THE MAELSTROM

She will go in.
Her blood will be sucked into a tube,
tested for what unwholesomeness exists;
her bones exposed on cold plates to colder eyes.

She will go out.
Words will hold her to books;
soap and water, to soiled laundry;
chopping boards, to the kitchen.

Time will slip over the edge of caution.

She will go,
her winter face carved exact as the time of day,
the blue wind tracing her seams.

*Jan. 15-20, 2007*

CANCELED FLIGHT

The night I approached the jay
his bead eye flicked and darted;
but oddly unstartled he turned
and allowed my stroke —
pure gloss beneath my hand.

Fearful of the dream's reality —
to touch a wild bird's wing —
I woke. But some dark interrupted sense
nagged me with its noise —
fluttering air or beating wing —
the unrealized joy of that baffling thing
unsought, unanswered, yet caught and cached.

What was measured from the mortal tick of him —
the velvet gleam, a gem of space —
the vivid blue of a different race?

Entrapped forever in the country of the dream,
did I stop or start a memory,
know a flash of second sight?
Or was I suddenly, brief as breath,
a strangely fashioned transmigrant.

*1980, Dunwoody*


THE SURVIVAL INSTINCT

First there is a warbling in the wires
such as the wind expresses,
then the splutter, the short circuit,
followed by a kaleidoscope of impressions
freezing and melting.

Time ebbs and resurges,
emptying debris
until there is only light,
the intensity of the blood,
and the ineluctable flash of response.

*June 27-29, 2003*

THE MIND TRICKS
(For Gay and the Logo)

The gryphons of the mind allow
acceptance without questioning.
What is strange can be as real
as anything familiar.

Fear comes later when one matures
and half of wisdom is common sense.
Creatures of the air don't couple
with creatures of the ground.
What good are wings that cannot soar
or feet that do not run?

Myths are born when gods are sought
to quicken fear or courage.
All that isn't can be what is.
The gryphons will insist.

*June 13-18, 2006*


THE LETTER NOT SENT
(from Lady Caroline to Lord Byron)

Dearest G
I shall not let the frost my heart feels seep
into this pen that writes so properly.
My feelings somewhere south of mind I'll keep
until the edge of loss has toughened me.
And if, my one-time dearest love, you care
to think of me, remember that I dared
to flout convention's shallow terms and wear
your love unshamed, the bond that once we shared.
You were my juggernaut. I cannot break
the rhythm of the days I spent with you.
Forgive the indiscretions for my sake
that there may be no bitter residue.
I wish you joy and marital success.
Your hands will touch this page —my last caress.

Most respectfully,
Caro

*March 19-25, 2001*

## VARIATIONS ON A PAINTING
(Portrait of Stellar's Jay)

Since I cannot free this jay
from its indecisive perch,
one leg tucked, eye bent on the possible,
I must bear the terrible guilt
of keeping a wild bird captive
on winter's stripped branch.

*Feb. 25-28, 2008*


## PORTRAIT OF STELLAR'S JAY 2

Lacking impertinence,
this jay frozen in uncertainty
seems no more than feathered brocade,
but as light flows in
embolding it, glossing its color,
I sense the heartbeat.

*Feb. 25 - Mar 2, 2008*


## BRAGGING RIGHTS

I am the small slug, earth-creeper,
below the level of human eyes.
Overlooked, mostly unseen, I lump about,
a fat dark finger the color of dung
trailing through the damp of morning,
munching my way through the prized petals
of lobelia and into the canna's leaves.
In my wake —destruction.

Flip me over.
My underside is unmatched
by any color in the universe.

*Aug. 1-3, 2008*

## STALKING

I hear him, the giant,
with that fee-fie-foe
and the thud thud
of his monstrous feet
even though I reportedly
downed him years ago.

He's out there
defying description,
absorbing space,
swallowing oxygen,
leaving me gasping for breath.

Every child knows my story—
Jack the Giant Killer—
fed like pap.
No one knows where he fell,
but without a body
there's no proof he's gone.

So every night I'm wielding my axe
chopping down the same bean stalk
waiting for exorcism that never comes.

*Feb. 1-5, 2011*


## INTIMATIONS

The sky is the color of old lace,
the roses' scent drifts around corners,
the Dachshund keeps fumbling the peanut in her mouth,
and the number of our days is extinguished like candles on a cake.

The fog's fuzziness blurs the birds,
the flowers reduce to a huddle of ghosts,
and the lights blear, too weak to reveal
what exudes such a cold, cold breath.

*June 21-26, 2005*

## THE SPIDER AT 9 AM

Just looking
you see where you traveled
leaving a track,
a taut springboard
for coming back
to breakfast on the unwary
enticed to dance upon it.

In the crotch of the rose bush
your silver castle
spun gray in the fog
waits,
studded with delicacies
you reach with one furry swipe
from your scrunched half-sleep.

Mornings are food for thought.
Preserved in silken wraps
are those who danced on air
now glittering in your trap.

*Feb. 1996*




## ONE LESS, ONE MORE

Another life has gone from mine.
The second of my Dachshunds lies
beside his sister in the earth,
pine cones circling both the mounds.
The simple crosses named and dated
will weather through the winter.
Forget-me-nots will bloom in  spring.

How long,
how brief
each breath of change;
the broken order of the days,
the spaces open in my heart,
the moon so late in the morning sky.

*Oct. 22-26, 1999*

## THE LIGHTS ARE UP; THE PLAY IS DONE

When I have shared another's skin,
I'm never free of it again.
I've closed the curtain on each one
but harbor portions of the sun
and shade that clothed and flooded me.
I've marketed humanity.

I hawked the best and worst of being
and wrinkled with the pain.
Yet every sinew, every bone
is strengthened by the tenancy
that harrows virgin ground and leaves
its gashes fertile, thirsty.

*March 10 - April 30, 1993*


## MORNING

The lordly crow
how he dominates
the very air
he flies in
whooshing masterfully
splitting silence into pieces.

*Oct. 23, 2012*


## REPEATS

There is only one whole dream
I am given again and again.
In the long nights it stretches,
its ungainly limbs usurping
the whole of the bed.

I watch myself
suspended out of existence
beyond the body's need of comfort,
hypnotized of necessity,
disappearing by choice.

*Oct. 22–30, 2009; April - May 23, 2010*

## JUST YESTERDAY

grief was for
a carelessly torn spider's web
a broken promise
an unkind word
a burned dinner
an inability to serve a need.

Just yesterday
tears were for
broken rose bushes
misunderstandings
being yelled at for being.

Just yesterday
your eyes shone with promise.

Just yesterday
you were here.

*1981, Dunwoody*


## NOT TOO LONG UNDER

Here's to morning:
The sunshine fingers inching in
bridging the bedshead,
traveling dizzy down my nose;
the summer sky swallowing the window,
lofting me on the cinnamon scent
of the fat red rose blooming nameless,
its sweet intrusion
crumpling the intellect.

I must time this briefest revel
a scant two minutes by the clock
or lose the pattern of existence
and never choose to wake again.

*Aug. 21-27, 1997*

171

INTERLUDES

PART I

With you, devious
grows insidiously
like cocoons
sprouting slowly
on pale afternoons.

Your magenta tones
pare through hair
crisp as morning bacon.

I'm quartered
by your long-boned
body, rived
by the red of your tongue.

The first bright pips
of morning sprout
like blossoms from a bough.

PART II

Down, down, down
the brink of years we slash
with splits of dreams:
children's mouths
ever aware against the night;
and strange dark beds
in old lost towns
where love and tomorrow
never quite equate.

PART III

Edges turn, heist,
eager at the asking.
Imagination is lost
in this alien setting
of two brown bodies
in a pool of sun
at the high of night.

Thirst and hunger know no shades
(afternoon's no brighter).
No willfulness is held in trust.
I'm boned beneath your trunk.

## PART IV

Pare the fell of feeling;
Slice the pelt of self;
hone the home of parroting.
Feast upon the wealth.

Garner every savoring
of joy and pain and ill.
I'm in love with nothing.
Day cries on the sill.

Covert-overt marries.
Dreams have broken frames.
Damn you! I wear crutches;
you have frozen veins.

## PART V

You've milked the sop
of giving and drained
it dry as hair.
I flow upon a desert
— drown in my despair.

Let me in; be Adam.
Blame me for what
you dare.
Anything is better
than bones and shanks
gone bare.

*March 15-16, 1972*


## LEILANI, THE FOURTH DACHSHUND

Her eyes go to far fields
impossible to track.
But contact or its lack
communicates
when you've been there before
with life spluttering out,
fires banked,
ashes imminent.

*July 25 – Aug. 6, 2006*

## NOVEMBER SIDE TRIPS

A trickle of birds,
an arpeggio of wings,
preludes the morning.

A little heaven
in the mauve blossoms of clouds
compromises dark.

Rain thunders, snapping
the stem of the final rose.
Petals clothe the earth.

Now the fog dilutes
the last of autumn's color.
One shroud and it's gone.

*Nov. 29 - Dec. 1, 2002*


## IN SEQUENCE

There's the first iris,
its portals open
to the great velvet room,
entrance to the castle.

I linger, thinking
leave a little for tomorrow
in this shimmering bloom,
but words get cheapened
in the blue of late spring.

A fat slug oozes toward delirium –
so much to feed on.
I trowel it off the stem
and flip it over the fence,
watch the tardy dew trembling
under the growing warmth,
and wonder if the dream I left
in the iris will melt.

*May 17 - June 18, 2007*

JUST SO

If you were here, night would have color
and impulse no darkening.
The moon would shepherd her stars,
nested fledglings cheep happily,
the wind thread slowly through leaves and flowers.
This fluid silver pen you left
would not be in my hand but in yours,
writing the lie to the twenty-five years you were gone.

*Oct. 25-31, 2006*


RECALL

The clouds spooled, fluid,
and suddenly the moon slipped free
revealing the flocked white canopy
of a lone tree in a field
spilling a strange green serenity
of grasses— mint, olive, lime—
not for lying on but to inhale.

Then perhaps it was not the moon at all
that set this tree upon the wall of memory
but some old ghost roused from sleep,
shaking the torpor of measured time,
living again— exultant.

*July 10-15, 2010*


INSIDE/OUTSIDE

I am the blank corner,
the juxtaposition of blue and brown
where nothing is exhibited,
where two walls have come together
to shut me out.

*Feb. 17, 2001*

INTROSPECTION

There is a word for it—precise.
I severed, disconnecting trust
from what was always known as truth.

Since then, I've traveled
the glittering hall of loss.
Nothing else was ever dared —
not love, not hate, not joy, not pity,
nor even hope or misery.
I've stumbled numb, insensitive,
and read what I have written down
as someone else's conscious thought
that makes a fool of me.

*Dec. 28-29, 2012;  March 2-4, 2013*


PHONE CALL

Her "Hello" hung expectant,
trembling across the line —
a hiatus of hope.

"Margie," I said.

The anticipation fell
crackling through the wire,
her dissolution
bitter as an unripe peach.

I could not question:
I knew her hope.
Distance though divined by distance
must be kept.

*Aug. 18-26, 2001*

INTERCESSION

I have arrested death
in the startle of a cat
in the long-legged calendula.
Up like a strumpet, he crosses
atop the wooden fence,
his eyes honey pools
flooding me with a single glance.

His advantage gone,
he undulates
in one sinewy motion to the ground
and tromps into the escallonia,
scattering the footprints of birds.

*March 11, 1993*


INTERRING

After I buried the death
in the cold heart of summer,
you came back —
whether to confirm or deny
I could not tell.
I could only continue dissembling.

*March 18-20, 2003*


LEARNING

I dreamed I papered the room
with words my tongue could not articulate,
certain the house would voice what I could not.
But I forgot a dedication.
Turning back, I saw
Its lack made all the difference.

*Sept. 19-24, 2006*

LET ME HEAR YOU

Speak to me.
Paint it in words:
My grief will be encompassed
in a frame I understand.

Give me language for consolation—
harsh with consonants,
soft with vowels,
the relief of plosives,
the quiet of sibilants,
the intensity of diphthongs—
a full range of expression,
the heights and the depths.

I shall hear you.
I shall be comforted.

*June 14-17, 2000*


REPLETE

When marriage was new
we laid the Ouija board
between us on the couch
and asked our children's names
and number.

Now years away
again we ply
our dreams in silent glide
across the same old sun face,
the yes and no of end
and beginning.

Our wrists tire.
Fascination is but a silly game of chance
where spelled-out answers
hold no gilded promise.
Or, are we half-past opportunity,
steeped in shaping what we have
and looking through the funnel backwards?

*Circa 1973*

## OUTMODED

I am in my novitiate, lately
past the spring and summer
conventional time of mastership.
It's not that I dawdle
out of whim or in my fashion
but that I'm not particular about the rate of gain
or the evidence of show and tell.

I'll not humble in the broad and dizzy of yesterday
nor screen my pattern with the smoke of words today.

I'll bonnet the very pluck of sky,
June it forever, blossom-high,
scuttling down the morning sea of fog
from heaven to the shore of grass and sun.

And I shall be done—
journey over —
apocryphal
to the very nature of sum total.
Now trace me on the wheel of your pedantry:
One
Two
Three —
Out goes she.

*June 21, 1975*


## IN-BETWEEN

The middle country, the interim
between awake and asleep,
has no bounds of time and space.
What occurs in that strange vale
haunts the mind until
it cannot free unreal from real.
Images move and events play out
as plausibly as a daily round.

You rouse, turned counterclockwise,
an alien, disengaged,
pursued by your own question—
"Where is it that I am?"

*July 23-26, 2004*

IN THE DARK

Sometimes at the height of the dream you waken,
the room unfamiliar, the present untenable.
Give me back the dream you demand.
But like all yesterdays it has gone
into one of many closed rooms,
identical but unmarked.

Stumbling at each threshold,
revelation trembling on the other side of the door,
you ask, "Is this it?" —
remembering those other turnings in the dark,
attempts at orienting,
spasms of glottal stops
before you learned to frame the question.

*June 9-13, 2004*


LET ME INTRODUCE YOU

Open your mouth.
I give you death
by the teaspoonful.

Come on, there's a good girl.
It goes down easily
once you've accommodated
the measure to your tongue.

Here, I'll support you
with my arm, your head
tucked to my chest.
Wider, please.

Swallow, swallow.
There. Now,
that wasn't so bad,
was it?

*Nov. 4, 1992*

## HIS SHIRT

After he died
his red and black
plaid shirt,
one sleeve
rent diagonally,
became mine.

Of course
it was too large
but the imprints
left by his shoulders
and the length of his arms
took up the space
that I couldn't.

*Feb. 17, 2001*


## ANALYZING

That love makes the world go round
implies that it endures and encompasses.

Why not love makes the world go
with the how and where unpredictable —
like go to hell and back,
like go square, intractable,
go crazy, irrational,
go morose, embittered?

Because that would not be pretty;
no one would commit it to memory
or slap it like frosting on a cake
to one who thought love was his alone.

*Feb. 3, 2013*

PASSAGES

Under ground
the dark things tunnel,
pushing earth
to the surface,
skewing tulips,
the purple smoke tree,
the fuchsias.
"Juicy Fruit gum will get 'em," says the neighbor.

"Try mothballs," says another.

"Forget that," says the gardener.
"Find the hole,
spoon in poison,
smooth off the top.
That works."

The nurseryman laughs
at all those enticements.
"Castor oil! They'll poop themselves to death."

I think of the labyrinths
full of warm furry things
shaped to their homes,
adapted.
They keep to their own quarters.
But we —warm or cold —invade theirs.

*March 13-17, 2001*


RESIDUALS FROM SYLVIA: NO PROMISES TO KEEP

The moon hides.
Mice whisper in the walls,
connive in the shadows.
A mossy sleep tames the wayward eyes.
A thin red keening in the skull
severs the thready breath.
All that is becomes what was.
What is alive was dead.

*Feb. 4-7, 2004*

## RETRENCHING

The wind ballooned from the hollow,
the river slurped, tasting its murky banks,
the fell of the moon crisped in the cold.

The house shrank
and she too grew smaller
cocooned under the blankets,
all around a ticking,
sloughing,
stirring.

She inhaled the dust of old dreams
and turned inside out like a pocket.

*Dec. 9, 1995 - Jan. 17,1996*


## WHOSE NAME RIDES THE AIR?

What wakes in the still dawn
and howls out a name?
What stifles the consonants
to make it unknown?

The game is forever,
taut as a tongue
that sleeps on the teeth
its message unsung.

The wind worries backward,
butts out of the eaves.
The syllables lengthen;
the word is a sword

that hones on the brain.
"Aeiou," it shrills;
"aeiou," it pales.
Then barren as morning
it's gone.

*April 19-20, 1994*

## NOISE POLLUTION

The dandelions are shrieking,
their petals in spikes.
There is so much yellow noise
the sun is forced from its dreamy cloud
to blast its rays at the disturbance.

How quiet the clamor.

*Feb. 27-28, 2010*

## SEPTEMBER

The fog melts, tardy
under the warming sky.
The mourning dove
plaintive on the wing
unsettles the emerging day.

*Sept. 13-16, 2012*

## BLOOD-BOUND

The barn swallow, uncertain,
whirring on the wire,
builds no nest in winter
even though the white azalea is blooming,
the rhododendron purple-tipped,
a fuchsia splashing red
and rows of grape hyacinth
bobble under a warm sun.

Does the worm taste no different in December
or are the senses so smothered by instinct
the ephemeral doesn't matter?

*Dec. 18-27, 1996*

## SEAM ALLOWANCE

I begin out of air to fashion
the here and now to live,
but the past bunches up, uneven,
and wrinkles what I form.

Grief is the thread that holds
the seams I lay together.
Joy eases out, puckers
between the narrow stitches.

The measuring stick is timeless
nicked by every slice;
the fabric cut on the bias
to minimize the give.

Because the thinnest scrim
separates us from each other,.
joy is patterned singly.
Yet grief makes you my brother.

*Aug. 27-29, 2002*


## IN WAITING

Ominous
still
with each knock
at the door,
the wolf,
grayer now,
less menacing,
persists.

"Let me
come in
the better
to know you."

*April 9, 2004*

## COMING OF AGE

When you suddenly turn seventy-two,
the sky is wider than the moon is blue.
You sweep your lives down the cobwebbed stairs
into the dustpan readied for years.

The scent sneaks in and worries your throat
and your gorge rises up like the raggedy coat
that you wore for years because it fit
the tempo and style you demanded of it.

The crow dips by in its mourning dress
with a thwack of wings, a sharp digress.
The wind roars out of the spacey hollow
and slaps the breath into your tomorrow.

*May 18-20, 2001*


## PREDESTINED

It's too early for frost,
that pearly breath
that rimes the harvest
of leaves and fruit.
The sun still rings
the golden coins
of alder leaves,
and wind-fall apples
tether in the grass.
But, premature,
one brown death among the firs,
stark in frozen loveliness,
betrays the careful symmetry of fall.

*Oct. 17-31, 2003*

## FOR THE TIME

For the time being is all I ask:
Tiptoeing to the east room
where the moon carved into the sky
proclaims its reign
spilling light into the corners.
For the time, being may be enough.

*Sept. 2006 - Aug. 2007*


## POINT OF DEPARTURE: THE PLAYGROUND

The long climb to the top of the ladder,
the swoosh down —
how quickly it goes
until at the bottom
one split- second pause
before the lift-off from earth
where you began.

*Sept. 1993*


## ROGUE WAVE

"Run!" he cried.
Over the dry sand we raced
until finally, bumbling frantically
jumping the driftwood piles,
we clawed into the side of the bluff.

It took the whole beach
chortling and shouting,
snapping and hissing,
thumping the logs over and over
inches below our feet—
a wild sweep of music,
the sirens' song of invitation
that I am afraid to hear again.

*1990's*

## THE LATE VICTORIAN

Here your words lie sleeping
under the wince of pain
among filmy scarves and rhinestones
and a single orange glove.

My hands move into shadows
to touch the ancient page,
my fingers igniting from old coals
on the scars of latent rage.

An agonizing show of courage
grew quietly through the years.
Anger now warms the very blood
once frozen by acceptance.

*Oct. 29, 1997*


## A TANGIBLE CALENDAR

Tucked in this corner, I half-sleep,
my face on the creamy softness of percale
so worn it betrays itself
by sprouting holes.

Forty years ago this pillow case was new,
ironed after every wash,
later trimmed with pink crochet.
Child of the Depression,
I cannot discard it,
make rags of what is yet serviceable.

My history builds.
I steep in the familiar—
the used, the faded, the scarred,
savoring what time leaves me.
It is how I mark my days.

*June 12-15, 2003*

EVERY FLOWER HAS ITS MIMIC

My flower beds are full of thieves,
weeds
that steal the identities of nurtured blooms
and mock the eye and evade the hand
that seeks to undermine them.

A dandelion well may be
a zinnia in miniature,
but only if an innocent eye
squints against the sun.

*Feb. 1-2, 2002*


THE THOUSAND DAYS

She had painted a face on canvas,
the eyes veiled  over horror,
the mouth squeezed
tight as a frozen bud.
Ghastly.

"Get rid of it," she said.
"I don't like to look at it."

The brows were hers,
the hair,
the contour
of cheeks and jaw.

I buried it behind the closet door.

Seasons passed,
enough to number
a thousand days
before she came again.
When she raised her eyes to me,
dear God,
I blanched to see the accuracy
of whatever vision, prophecy
had somehow moved her hand to trace
the future canvas of her face.

*Oct. 27 - Nov. 2, 1995*

OCTOBER 26, 2008

Especially now October gleams
with frosty dew across the fields
and weeds blade silver under morning sun.
Dogs and people expand their senses
and sniff in the promises of intent
a chill north wind suggests.
It is time to hunker, sweep out the spent,
prepare for what is different.


SUSPENSION

I have filled these earth cups
with life in abeyance,
bulbs in dry brown shells;
clothed them in mature compost
sluiced with water.
Now I shall wait.

Fall and winter will shrivel petals,
scatter leaves, lay down frost.
Maybe as early as January
green candles will emerge,
little nubbins of delight
splaying out in bold verticals,
support for tear-shaped cradles.

Days will move slowly,
the sun warm the air.
I shall wait,
the heart and eyes twin studies,
for fifty red tulips to flare,
birthday after birthday.

*Sept. 1994*

## A LITERAL TRANSLATION

Spring wakes with sunrise
in the garden, in the heart.
Nesting birds chirp away
the night of wind and rain
that stripped the painted daisy of its petals.


## A SUB-TEXTUAL TRANSLATION

She sleeps but wakes at first light,
her journey just begun. The doctor waits,
his hands like cups, to catch the silky head.
One clap, one startled shriek
assaults the icy air.
"Little bird, little bird," the mama says,
"You've pushed the night away.
"Neither rain nor wind could stop
this flowering of my heart."


## A MELDED TRANSLATION

Spring pre-empting sleep, I wake at dawn
in another place, another time, to a seagull's keening cry.
Night gone with its wind and rain,
I count the petals of the early rose,
spilled blood upon the ground.

*June 4, 2005*


## LITTLE WHITE LIES

Snow-in-Summer —
that rush of bloom
in five doubled petals
each lashed black
to a chartreuse eye —
not accurately named,
but perhaps the observer
white-blinded
missed the singular.

*May 3-8, 2011*

## SOAPSTONE SCULPTURE, SECOND STREET GALLERY

A mother lap
and a tiny head
is only the obvious.

I long to crawl
into that capacious lap
circled by those mammoth arms;
be warmed by the patina of antiquity
inherent in the stone
and absorb the mystery
of the creation;
understand why
the head must be so small —
inconsequential really —
and the body
an affirmation of excess.

*Nov. 19-30, 1998*


## SMOKE AND MIRRORS

Only innocents see ghosts
drifting in with gentle grace
soft as dust, blurred by space.
Fear nor thought attend their passage;
doors nor chairs impede their way.
Whatever is their cache of knowledge
wraith-like disappears with day.

Only innocents see ghosts,
charcoal  smudgings for their features;
friends that wake when others sleep,
companions for their night adventures.

All we others weight our visions,
let them loom as nightmare creatures,
fearful omens of coming doom,
reminders of our ancient sins
sprouting horns in some bad dream.
Only we jaded create in depth
ghosts of conscience, the primordial scream.

*Sept. 19-30, 1998*

## A SONNET FOR GAY WHO ASKED FOR ONE

The bee lay drunk with sleep inside the rose
before the sun and wind could quicken day —
in perfect mimicry of death his drowse —
bent wings, scrunched legs in startling disarray.
Yet I have seen my own in tumbled rest,
my children, bottoms up, arms splayed for flight
to Oz or Eden, leaving me bereft,
clutched tight, shocked cold, identified with night.
Is choice ordained, the sleep of life or death,
the moment measured by the clock —or not?
We move through loss of longing, lack of mirth,
the sullied past in which we're always caught.
When all for which I yearn and dream slips free,
it is my hope that death will summon me.

*Nov. 2-12, 2000*

## SMALL VICISSITUDES

The wild iris,
the wild fuchsia
bare their gratitude
graciously.

Color does not leak
from them
nor height shrink
under the quiet rain.

Beneath the eaves
winged creatures flicker
damply hopeful
for the drying wind.

Silence waits
out of range,
the rain soft,
indistinct as a heart beat.

*June 30 - July 6, 2012*

## THE DEAD DON'T SHARE

In century-old houses the rooms are so filled with presence
you draw in your shoulders to conserve space.
You keep your hands close to your body,
extending the fingers to palp the air.

What you know of hunger feeds on possibilities:
You mouth, "Who is there?"

Old dreams circle, the dust raw in your throat.
The windows of rippled glass reflect only your distortions
until all who lived here, interbound, crowd you out.

*May 12-17, 2009*


## TO FEED A HUNGER

Over the wave's sough
the gull's cry is distinctive,
fluttering down the air
and breaking in pieces on the sand.
I have waked to those particles of sound,
remembering.

Once with loaves of bread
that did not rise well,
I planted myself on the shore
and hoarsely croaked at the sky
until, singly first,
then like an approaching storm
the tiny thunder of wings magnified
and all around me were gulls,
their waxen bodies glinting
like jewels under glass.

*Dec. 16-28, 1996*

194

EITHER/OR

What will it be?
The complexity of dandelions,
the simplicity of clover,
an invasive patch of vetch or gorse,
a hurdle to scramble over?

Will the season finish turning,
the clouds tumble in disarray
to keep the sun from slipping through
for one more day?

Everything is far too much
or my vision is too narrow.
My nightly dreams are camouflage
for the reality of tomorrow.

*Aug. 16-17, 2003*


EASTER SUNDAY, 2005

How must it be
cocooned,
wrapped so closely
the contours of the body evident,
the shroud falling away,
emerging in a different form
winged and colorful as a butterfly
or radiant as the Christ?

*March 27, 2005*


FRUITLESS

I am who I am
but sometimes I'm not.
I've hidden in one of my pockets,
greedily sopping up the essence
of the world going by,
seeking the apple of contentment
from a tree that cannot bear.

*Dec. 25-31, 2000*

## TESTING THE FIRMAMENT

Clouds sieved between me
and morning blue
suggest there is a different hue
on some unknown horizon,
that if I rouse and properly sift
layers of pain
from irrelevant thought,
blue won't be black
in some false state
of grief and guilt.

Wincing from the rush of light,
stripped of inconsistent faith,
I shall see with unveiled eyes
that God's mercy comes disguised.

*July 11-22, 1996*


## LAST RIGHTS

When you come
after the long journey
to the final crossroad,
you turn left hoping it's right
because right has mostly been wrong.
Yet you keep going
and the road narrows
to rhododendrons brushing you on one side
and gorse on the other.

You know to turn around,
twisting the wheel to right and left,
bruising your car forward with flowers,
backwards with spines,
until you can face the way you came.

*Dec. 28-29, 2004; Aug. 16-18, 2005*

ROUNDS

What is left of summer lies,
disguised
by miles and miles
of graybeard grasses,
white-haired dandelions,
and dry-mouthed pods
toothy with seeds
black, yellow, and brown.
The smallest of breaths
will give them loft.
New earth will mother.

All that lives
just simply moves
from drowse to drowse,
wrinkled infancy to wrinkled age.
Nothing is as once it was.
Yet nothing's lost;
it's only changed.

*Aug. 1-5, 1998*


STRETCHING

The night has grown so tall
it has pushed through the ceiling,
outgrowing this small room,
the back corner of the house.

It must be reaching
for the moon, the stars,
to illuminate its purpose
by sheer contrast.

*Aug. 6-9, 2009*

## HALLOWEEN RAIN

is eyeballs oozing down the window pane
popping apart one atop the other
making of horror a wet slur.

Halloween rain
is dancers tapping and sliding down
onto their former partners
in a grotesque semblance of love.

*Oct. 24-30, 2006*


## DESIRE OF THE MOTH

The other person is always there
creating discord in palpable air.
He splits up marriages,
takes the sheen from love,
instilling disaster wherever he goes.
But, worst of all, he lies in wait
behind your reflection in the glass,
distorting your reasoning,
awakening your doubt,
questioning your sincerity,
then blotting you out.

*July 31, 2000;  Sept. 26, 2003*


## SET IN STONE

I want to go somewhere.
Anywhere.

No, you don't.

The sun, moon, clouds
go somewhere, anywhere.
Somewhat indeterminate,
ungoverned,
they're allowed.

You're allowed the want.

*Sept. 25-26, 2012*

## SOMETHING LOST

Somewhere there is a house
that appeared in my dreams.
I do not know what it holds,
only that I need to enter it.

Once on a road trip
I saw that house
and felt the whole astounding
memory of it flood me.
I did not dare tell the driver
that he had to go back.
He would never have understood
that there was something there for me.

The house remains trapped.
I no longer dream of it
and I have no idea where it is.

*Sept. 18-19, 2004*


## SPRING NIGHT

In the woebegone hours
the dark seels me
until the moon unveils
like a slippery fish
darting in and out of the clouds
playing peep-eye with the universe;
the birds twirp, mothering their featherless chicks;
and the frogs in the south pond
brup, brup in their signature E-flat.

Then I'm unstitched, raveling out,
loosed to the warm night —
free to go where I couldn't,
free to go where I will.

*May 21-25, 2002*

IMPASSE

Here I am
with your too-real smile
and a plastic clock that keeps
good time where it should —
on the face of things.

My wishes bend
to accommodate yours
and tick and tock
are endless cues
that regulate
the turn of screws.
What was bright
and what was fair
leaves no residue to share.
Wormless is the flesh of things
but nothing rots
and nothing stings.
Time is jointless
outside age;
but love devoured by bitter rage
can only detonate.

*Dec. 27, 1973*


CLOSING BOOK

Time to close with a crisp snap.
It is finished —
the plot, the sequence
absorbed by silence.
Only the characters remain
to be rejuxtaposed in the sequel:
Who will stride forward, who will be cowed.

*Aug. 2009*

## BETWEEN TIDES

Three months I searched the tide line
on beaches where you had never walked.
With newborn greediness I seized
the treasures the ocean spewed:
agates, jasper, worm-eaten wood,
shells and fossils of shells.

It was not enough.

Minus tides exposed the world
forgotten the years of inland living:
purple and orange starfish, swollen askew;
bursts of green-fleshed anemones;
uncompromising shells of chiton, armor-dark.

Yesterday the young man,
tennis shoes suspended from his neck, stopped.
"Today's my birthday."
Looking up, raising his hands, he said,
"I asked God to please get me to Bandon safely."

He showed me a snakeskin agate just found,
a red jasper with a quartz band,
jingling his pockets with their collection
"for my friend who tumbles rocks."
Peeping into my bucket, he observed, puzzled,
"You go for the colored ones."
Then, smiling clear up into his eyes,
he swung away,
praising the Creator with his joy.

*Oct. 12, 1983*


## OUT IN LEFT FIELD

The shortest questions plague me –
when, where, why, what, who.
A monosyllabic query
requires a polysyllabic slough
of words that amuse or confuse,
a wilderness I find appalling.
No wonder my eccentric muse
resorts to dismal mewling.

*July 2000*

## BROKEN SLEEP, BLIND SEER

The fetal curl is gone, unwound
by the prickle against the senses.
Night offers only a surface sleep,
a rise and ebb of consciousness.

Near and far like marauding flies
images buzz the brain.
East turns west and west turns east
on vaguely familiar terrain.

And I am lost like blind Tiresias
blundering to interpret
by sound and touch and scent and taste
what may prove to be irrelevant.

*July 30 - Aug. 4, 2002*


## DEAR MORPHEUS,

Here is the borrowed dream,
the one you lent me when I was eighteen.
I am returning it, intact, unrealized.
You will forgive me I'm sure if I say
it wavered in and out of my conscious like a mirage,
that the more I struggled to reach it,
the farther away it got.

I am no longer in thrall:
I don't live here anymore.
I hope you'll understand.

Gratefully,

Mary

*Feb. 4, 9, 2008; July 4-5, 2010*

## A STUDY OF THREADS

I live on borrowed afternoons
stockpiled years ago.
Guilt runs through these stolen hours,
a thin black thread I pull
to gather up unmeasured days,
cinch neatly every seam.
Then I grimace for what I see
are wrinkles and puckers
and nothing of me.

*Oct. 6, 1997*


## SLIVERS AND HALVES

The new moon lies
thin as a smile
I've known too many of —
the ones you don't return
because they disappear
into pursed lips,
something the moon's can't do
because it has no cupid's bow.

It hangs there
night after night
getting thicker and thicker
until it turns
into a cartoon mouth,
flat across the top.

It's still a smile, of course,
but it alienates me.

*May 3-6, 1998*

CONTRAST

The uncertain dark
noses the glass
like a child
waiting to come in,
the pressure of hope
bold enough
to rouse the mother
to feel a wish
to open the door
to welcome the night
with one quick glance
at the swirl of stars
before she trips the switch.

*Aug. 25-27, 2000*


SHORT SHRIFT

Such a little scar,
plump as a pillow,
feather-edged.
Reminds me
of good-bye kisses
from pursed lips
blown off the fingers,
not intended for the recipient
but a show for the crowd.

Perhaps then this scar
was unintended,
an interruption
in the smooth flow,
a pock upon the flesh
unerringly struck
but not the target.

*Jan. 10-12,  2003*

## NO FEAR

A little shudder in the trees
a tremble in the bud
a hissing rush against the grass
clouds swallowing the sun

two moans between the house and wall
a growling in the logs
kissing smacks upon the glass:
— the wind escorts the rain.

*May 2001*


## YESTERDAY'S PROMISES

These are last year's seeds on the warm sill,
forgotten promises enclosed in plastic
between damp paper towels,
each a tremble of anticipation,
a potential of sprout.

Tomorrow has not come.
I do not live in hope—
it may never come—
but dutifully
I slip the curtain aside
to check for viability.

There are beads of moisture,
plumped-up skins,
a whisper of affirmation
that what is nourished in a vacuum
without hope, without passion;
what's inherent in the past
may yet be brought to flower.

*Sept. 2, 1998*

## A SUIT OF CHROME

She was unsuited
to that time,
that place,
so that leaving
was neither solace
nor retreat.

She returned,
an assault,
her armor in place,
brilliant as chrome.
She dazzled the dimwits
with charm in her scorn
and laughed herself sensible
all the way home.

*Feb. 23-25, 2001*


## SUN AND SHADE

Impossible to sleep
with growling consonants,
wailing vowels,
hissing sibilants .

They gloat
as they mesh and separate,
hide in labyrinths,
horn out in lush cornucopias.

I reach into the indiscriminate,
compose a phrase, another,
feeling the sun shine in my brain.

Then all tumbles smirking
into disparate zones
outside my map of reference.

*Aug. 25 - Sept. 13, 2010*

# WINTER SOLSTICE

Waxen with frost the wild strawberry,
darkened with cold the slug
matching the sodden leaves of the calla lily,
but perky robins are gleaning sustenance,
white clouds bubble in and out,
squirrels arc from pine to pine.

The night skies prickle with stars
and the half-moon's
half grin is smugly luminous.

*2009*


# RESPONSES

Where are you going?

Out.

Where have you been?

Around.

Nothing ever changes —
always the cold rain
slicing vertical patterns
down the jaw bone,
into the neck's hollow,
along the shivering spine,
knifing through the thighs and calves,
and finally to the ground.

Chilled, immobile,
except for the sheltered tongue,
where am I going?
Out.

Where have I been?
Around.

*Aug. 8-11, 2002*

## THE CACHE

I struggled
to absorb what fed me
springing from the music
whispering from the walls,
but I had reached
the saturation point
unconsciously.

There has to be more,
the yearning lingering,
the hunger insistent.
Or, maybe I swallowed  yesterday
with all my senses blunted.

*Dec. 18, 2012 - Jan. 3, 2013*


## CROWING

Good morning, crow.
You must be old
because the pine  branch above
grays your sheen.

You pick  at rough bark
with no enthusiasm,
your desultory glance my way
barely  discernible.

Blasé, you loft and wing
in one swift motion
to the rooftop, soundless
in your possession of space.

*July 20-22, 2012*

## AUTUMN

This season shrivels,
forcing immediacy.
Time is going halt.

Tomorrow, one year
on the calendar I keep,
flashes and snuffs out.

A gulosity
consumes me. I droop, sated
with indiscretions.

*Nov. 8-11, 2001*


## THE LONG SHADOW

Captured in this photo,
Uncle George, Aunt Vivian,
Bessie and John
squint into the Southern sun.

One shadow, amorphous,
usurps the foreground,
nibbling and swallowing
the four pairs of feet.

Who thinks far ahead ,
when that family long dead,
reviving the time and revoking the place
that no one would know the photographer's face?

*Jan. 9-20, 2002*

TWO-FACED

The days of slushy clouds ooze by;
the night drops in with chips of ice.
The year's first month is Janus' s call:
Go forth, go back. It's winter, it's fall.

A single rose in the naked bush
blooms beautiful in perversity.
Yet, here I stand in the filmy dark
mouthing again the childish plea:
"Sparkle, sparkle, little twink,
'who in the hell are I you think?"

*Jan 7-9, 2011*


TO SLEEP, PERCHANCE TO DREAM

A sting of wind,
the thrust of rain:
I willed my eyes to sleep again.

My hands went flat.
The day slept late.
The bee in the bonnet refused to wake.

So tardy I with latent thought,
delayed reaction to the old dog's bark
and the silent tick of the electric clock.

Morning should come
not soon but late,
for dreams are richer
the final hour,
the honeyed hive,  the last hurrah
before the day takes over.

*May 11-14, 1999*

TO BE

If I could milk the blood
from the written page
to bring to life a character
who on the stage has weight and substance,
the reality
that draws the dreamer from his shell
that wakes the stifled  from his sleep
that rouses seeming lethargy
to laugh, to think, to weep,
I'd use the right of mime and stance,
supplying breath to given words,
to wear the panoply, the guise,
to be someone I never was.

*July 16-20, 2003*


UNSIRED DREAMS

I sleep as if possessed by dream.
My nights are strangely peopled
by fiction makers, journal keepers
of lives I've never lived.

Yet I am lord of paragraph
who shapes their diction, makes them laugh
and recreates their splendid posture
large as nightmare, strange as life.

I am a ravenous mother of dreams
that feed on me in swollen night.
Nurture is my private thief
whose loot I cache in rhymed relief.

By daylight, I am barren.

*1970*

## THE LONG ACCEPTANCE

Between the known and possibilities
the gulf is wider than the mind
can stretch to comprehend a death.

Do I outrun the longing arms of grief
to call a halt to questioning the why
and let the sun indifferent diffuse my pain?

If so, then I will be an element
unknown on any chart devised by man,
denied the right of trial by fire or ice.

*May 6-17, 2003*


## KNOWING COLORS

Color is identified early.
That's red.
That's brown.
That's green.

The enrichment comes later
to bloom in the darkest recesses ,
its intensity never lessened —
the blood red,
the chocolate brown,
the cypress green.

*Oct. 30 - Nov. 26, 2006*


## THE SPOILER

I know you.
You sit there in the anonymity of crowds
and rain a little doubt on my parade.

I staunch whatever emanation comes
to bleach the joy I refuse to trade
for your flat discordant horns and muffled drums
and that endless tune you hum through narrowed lips.

*Aug. 2 - Dec. 5, 2003*

UNRESOLVED
(To My Son)

The mind wears shadows.
Night breaks out its stars and moon
luminous and raw.
October hones its edges,
ragging the pattern of loss.

Petals rip, stalks sway
under the hammering wind.
Earth steeps in puddles
cresting with waves of spun rain
forcing autumn to abort.

I winter. The past
smudges the premature dawn
bringing tomorrow
before I spend my today
throbbing against your absence.

*Oct. 16-31, 2000*




IS IT TIME

It is only the clock that weights the hours.
Beneath the brackish light of day,
the earth sodden with sleep,
the flowers under rain protect the colors
in their wrinkled shrouds.

Impatient with the tardy sun,
I lift the crinkled petals
to expose the throat.
The promise breaks;
the landscape sullied.
And, I, arrogant trespasser,
have lost the realm of anticipation;
peeled down a little life
for one small tick of time.

*Aug. 25-28, 1993*

TROCHEES IN SQUEAK
(Speaking Squeak)

All the little squeaks are magnified
here among the silent sounds of words
scrabbled on the page undignified.
Yet by editing they're minimized.

Small or big they speak euphonically
planned to rise and fall with studied art.
Head to tail they're juxtaposed to speak
Squeak, the ultimate of language shock.

*Feb. 1-4, 1999*


THE WASH

There are things I would write,
but my pen runs thin
for the wind carries autumn
when the need is for spring.

There are things I would do,
but my mind is afloat,
the hours too timeless
to anchor in thought.

One part of me drowses,
the other's aloft —
the dichotomy endless,
the reason in doubt.

So I drift without snags
on the surface I know
but am tied to the dark,
the unknown below.

*Sept. 12-15, 2002*

## THE SOUND BARRIER

We can do nothing more for you the doctor said.
But who ever can do more
than patch to make a sum of parts.

The mind accepts matters to attend,
passages to explore:
on the quiet board of memory;
dealing with silence
forever burring like insects on a summer night,
toneless as the river's drift,
static as a stopped clock.

*April 20- 29, 2006*


## WRINKLERS

I would be old
but it's too early in the day.
Some timid longing keeps surfacing
as poetry becomes prose with age,
as what loomed tall shrinks,
as today is but tomorrow magnified.

The decades counted, multiplied by seven,
have swallowed all the platitudes once glibly mouthed.
It may be time to go,
but the heathen child refuses.

*July 21- Aug. 6, 2007*


## SLOW DRIFT

There's no crackle left in my mornings:
I'm webbed in a giant clutch.
Over me rides the sunshine,
under me shadows twitch.

I will take years to unravel
under the merciless light,
to fall slowly, free as wind drift,
into the lap of night.

*Oct. 28-29, 1997*

MIRED

Maybe there's nothing else to say—
words dried leaves
scudded into corners,
piled up, meaningless.

Maybe there's an exhaustion of the senses
reliable for decades.

Maybe anticipation was buried yesterday,
worn out waiting.

Maybe, just maybe,
It has all been said.

*May 1-3; 6, 2004*

# FLOWERING

BANDON BEACH

It's virgin soil you walk
on the sea-scarred sand
and virgin it will be
when you return.

Farther out the rocks
carved into the shapes of legends
wear their own  eternity,
>            a face lifted to the sky,
>            a cat hunkered with her kittens,
>            the overturned basket from which they escaped,
>            the huge dog, his muzzle rested between his paws,
all waiting
for belief to make myth reality.

Perhaps it does.
The beach keeps its secrets.
No one can read what the waves wrote
last night at high tide.

*Aug. 23-29, 1998*


ASSESSING THE PLATEAU

A slow insidious thing,
this counting backward,
knowing it will never be over,
no rising from the stupor
to bask in the sun,
to border on a dream.

It is all yesterday,
staying raw,
measuring losses,
holding the years on my lap
to keep them warm.

*Oct. 25 - Dec. 15, 1994*

## AFTER YESTERDAY, TIME

I'm telling time again
and you can take it from me, old buddy,
at your discretion.
In those hollows where I nestled or wallowed,
days didn't count
and there never was a next year
I had to think about.

How greenly I grew through spring and summer,
and when fall began to tint me, I scarcely noticed
for I kept you captive by my children's birthdays.

Out of children now, I know impending frost
blackening my flowers,
whiting out the ground cover,
making brittle bones of spent stems;
the soft wilt when the sun touches,
melting down my years to a formless gray.


## AS I THINK, AM I

I'm being defeated by words
on the ninth of October,
plucking all the hopeless ones:
drear
dull
lethargic.
What if I were
to peel from their pages
perky
shiny
brisk
and toss them
like orange purple red leaves
into the air;
watch them loft, soar
and drop their colors to the ground?
I could crunch them underfoot
and revel in their fragments;
scoop them up
juggle them
sift them through my fingers;
and, memorizing their shapes,
carry them into November.

*Oct. 9-13, 1993*

## VALLEY WOMAN: DAMMIT, INSIDJUS MAC

I feel like I'm meltin' down.
Oh, I ain't losin' any flesh,
jest slowly disappearin'.

It's like my brain forgot
how to make sense
and all those words I usta play with
jest hov'rin' there like a flock of birds
'n me with no crumbs to feed 'em.

*July 5-21, 1998*


## BOXED

Collector of boxes,
dust-rimmed portraits,
browned newspaper clippings,
you, slipping fishlike in and out of dreams,
taking sustenance blind-mouthed,
the senses bound in netting
cast to gather the jumble of the universe,
sense and nonsense blended,
wavering between worlds,
calling out for recognition
from either or both,
flattening time,
neither day nor night,
shrinking dimensions.

Only your smile remained the same
and the crinkling white of your hair.

*Dec. 23-29, 1995; Jan 3, 1996*

## BY THE SEA

Cease?
Desist?
As if one could command
his lungs, his heart, his senses;
put a stop to the known
and disappear into the unimaginable.

There are no quiet harbors
that pain has not drained dry.
But on small green islets
the senses alone know,
one can finger the lace
left by waves on the shore
and find it substantial.

*May 23-24, 2004*


## A CELEBRATION OF WEATHER

Wrung out with this June
that spells April by rain—
its winds from the south
that tattoo on the brain
by day and by night
in relentless refrain—
I steeped in the depths
of the paddies of grass
among petals of roses
the wind had torn loose—
strips of raw flesh
bulging up on the ooze.

Wet winds were not all.
The air flowed in sweet,
nothing like April
that trumpets defeat
of grim winter's onslaught
with quick bursts of bloom;
and drinks up the moisture,
reveling in gloom.
I'm really in clover
not under the weather,
for I don't have to water;
I don't need a broom.

*June 11-14, 2000*

## FINALE

A slur of rain,
a slash of wind —
the flowers pout
against a green
that's turning brown
in flattened curls.

November whirls
in tune with death —
a final swirl,
a pirouette,
a gracious bow,
an empty stage.

*Nov. 23-26, 2000*


## VALLEY WOMAN: BUMP ON A LOG

I bin thinkin' so much lately
I ain't no more than walkin' bones.
Here it is near to Christmas
'n I'm messin' 'round with last spring.
Got no more mind than a bunny rabbit.
Summer musta gone some place
but I cain't find none of it.

I'll jest git to goin' on dec'ratin'.
They say act like you got the spirit
even if you don't
and it'll eventually come back.

All I know is I don't wanna
wake up Christmas
thinkin' it's the Fourth of July.

## FOR THE MOMENT ONLY

the play's the thing:
The stinging life of words
climbs every mountain of faith
and hesitating,
hesitating,
falls into the sea of discernment.

The bulk of character spills
from shoulders, chin, brow
until who can say
whether Ed is Max or Max, Ed;
or here is here
or was is now.

The magic breaks like a skyrocket —
one moment against the dark —
into a thousand pieces of dream.

Strike the flats
Draw the curtain
Put out the lights.

*1987*


## WHAT'S BUGGING ME
(Chilly Fingers in July)

The slippage,
the hitches in time
bare me to the world
newborn –
with only a fear of falling
into unbroken sound,
with only a fear of falling
into a sea of light;
stripped down to the essentials,
battling to find what I know –
agape –
like a fish at the surface,
the depths churning murky below.

*2000*

GIVEN THE MOON

Seven years down.
Sadie, you do not know
the weight of years
pressing upon
your lonely bones.

It's I alone
who feel and know
the touch of rain,
each slippery stone;
the stars that pin
the night around;
the soft cream color of the moon
gone white in the approaching dawn;
the faintest flush of morning sun.

You made these simple pleasures mine.
Everything that you have been
is given over and over again.
You warm the earth I walk upon.
I never think of you as gone.

*Feb. 4-14, 1996*


FREE WITH TAX

No one pays for a poem.
It merely jolts the heart,
races the blood,
startles the eyes open,
electrifies the memory.

It holds old ghosts
of substance and revelation,
anoints you with understanding.

Accepted or not,
it will have its due.

*Feb. 27-28, 2010*

## VALLEY WOMAN: GETTIN' READY

Look how them leaves is startin' to curl up
gettin' ready to drop.
Funny how nature works
sose nothin' happens overnight:
They's always a prep'ration for change.
Halfway through August
you can smell a diff'rence in the air,
a tap'rin' offa new growth.

I'm not sayin'  nothin's left to bloom
for they's mums and dahlias in the bud
and the fuchsias goin' crazy with color,
plus them hollyhocks aimin' for the sky,
their li'l skirts all poofed out like par'chutes.

No,  ma'am.
I'm just sayin' they's a long time
for gettin' ready to quit;
and if you got eyes to see,
all them signs are there
from August right up inta November.

*Oct. 11-12, 1999*


## FLYING

When you have wings, you fly,
the air embracing,
holding you up,
wind caroling in your feathers,
sun honey-sweet on your spine.

You glide,
you soar,
the throb of your wings a rhythmic heartbeat —
The joy is the journey.
You never arrive.

*May 10-14, 2006*

# THE GLASS DOOR

Again I heard
not the fingering wind,
the clink of rain on the glass,
not the heave of the wooden gate,
nor even the skip of branches along the house,
but the dog's soft paw against the door.
When I went as always to let him in,
only my reflection looked back at me
and expanding space curiously empty.

For years he has come with strange persistence
to pad at the door seeking entrance.
What need moves him to ask for me
then not be there when I appear?
Perhaps my need calls out to him;
my spirit roving, lost, unpatterned,
yearns for contact from his world.

In swift times and slow, darkness and day,
I have gone at the summons and met my own face,
puzzled, askew, a moue of surprise,
an explosion of senses oddly betrayed.

Because some quirk of vision, lack of insight
turns substance to space
knocking reason awry,
I face a bare glass and cannot see
who stands at the door and waits for me.

*Nov. 17-29, 1995*


# GRACE IN SMALL SPACES

Under the roof of December
shadows drown in shadows,
night trembles at the window,
and mortality asserts itself
like thunderclouds in May.

But the quiet fragments,
breaking into pieces of light,
and morning opens ablaze with primroses
to warm the little winters of the mind.

*Dec. 14-29, 2000*

227

GRANDDOG AND I

In the first green of spring
he lurched against me,
one eye a milky cup,
the other clear.
Blind-sided,
he tucked his head to see
the better part of life
and all of me
if I sidled in
to the seeing side.

Then suddenly the eye washed clear,
but much of what he'd seen before
was shadow now.
He'd butt his head into the door,
his nails a-clatter in nervous haste,
scuttling to find his dinner bowl.

As my dog ages, so do I.
The shadows grow peripherally.
We waver, stumble against the known
lost in ever narrowing paths
until  timing more than touch or vision
leads us where we want to go.

*March 26-28, 1999*


JANUARY 1, 2006

All news is yesterday's —
playbacks of the dire,
the frightful, the ludicrous,
the sinful, the gracious.

Roil while you revisit,
saturating yourself
in past miseries,
triumphs, and revelations.

Keep no time for today.
Survival requires
turning a blind eye
so that you never hear
the fat lady sing.

*Dec. 17, 2005 - Jan. 1, 2006*

## VALLEY WOMAN: BRUSH STROKE

"Write it down," she said,
"there on that paper
so's the old man'll know
I cain't go
scrubbin' the floors,
wrestlin' them heavy rugs,
and carryin' that fat dog
down the steps no more.

'slong as I'm on my feet
he's thinkin' I can do ever'thing
same as before.

"You gotta write it out
in black and white,
else he jest keeps expectin'
and never sees nothin' but yesterday."

*July 2-3, 1996*


## IF THE SALT HAS LOST ITS SAVOR

You offer me tomorrow.
I need look no farther than May
when, like fountains pent all winter,
everything erupts, flooding the senses.

The sky shrieks blue.
Clouds like gauzy petticoats
whisk past, barely skimming the wires
where birds, delirious, take their morning breaks.

And I with decades of spring behind me
feel each pore pucker
and the blood bubble in my veins.

With one full tilt I can swallow
the full draught of May
and emerge through the dark scrim of winter
totally inebriated.

*Feb. 2, 1993*

## IN THE FULLNESS OF TIME

In my own good time
I shall drink the rain.

When May slips into June again
and false fruit from false labor swells
to compromising bud,
the garner of the distant years
grown green with time
slides me down to zero base
to beg from every faded bloom
some smack of recompense.

When summer melts to autumn
in the full graciousness of time,
one single flower is absolution.
I shall drink the rain.

*May 6-8, 1996; May 7, 2006*


## A LITTLE LUNAR MADNESS

Come,
let us take the color of today's sky
to stain our bodies
so that we dance blue
under summer stars.
We need more
than a nodding acquaintance
with lunacy.

Let us keen in pitch
higher and more raucous
than the frogs in their sludge ponds;
stretch our arms and quiver like the frowzy shore pines;
invite the crows to perch atop our heads
and natter their menace at the universe.

We have been decorous too long,
have shrunk and shriveled like slugs
caught napping by the morning sun.

*June 25 - July 2, 1997*

# LIVING IN MURKY WATERS

I have become someone else,
grown like a Georgia O'Keefe flower
suffocating in its petals,
a study in brown
of frogs muted in their muddy pools.

Around my prison the secret rain
plops kisses on the glass
and the wind stealthily connives
with the spent leaves.

I have grown like Topsy to share
in equal portions shadow and sun
and see my whole world
like a collapsed circus tent
wrinkling in the dawn.

*Aug. 25, 1994; Jan. 1 - April 30, 1997*


# MORE THAN BONES

"Does that hurt?"
The fist thuds against my foot.
"No."
"Nothing broken then."

It's more than bones.
It's all those immeasurables
the heart and mind are prey to
assaulting for twenty-four thousand days
sense and sensibility,
separating and fusing
over and over again,
scar upon scar,
until pain is so diffused
the intellect shatters.

Does that hurt?
Yes.

*May 21-24, 1995*

## A LETTER NOT SENT

I'm not telling you, Mom,
that the old dog was put to sleep.
You would want the same.

Do not ask me for it.
I'd fall into a sea of salt
and be scrubbed down to bone.

I know you live there,
the heart of a great web
that spins out beyond my reach.

With bones too fragile,
the universe now your bed,
you tend yesterday's gardens
in a secondary land.

Yet, your mind
like faceted crystal
catches light,
reflects brilliance
into havens of dark;
and rouses to wrest
meaning from words.

No, Mom, I won't have
your eyes darken deeper blue;
nor break under the one-quarter smile
that I know would touch your mouth.

I'm not going to tell you.

*1993*


## MINOR OBSERVATION

It is easy to imagine your life a pie
three-quarters consumed,
one quarter left shriveling.

It is hard not to.

*Feb. 3, 2013*

OBITUARIES

Our time is up: We fall like dominoes.
One touch, the ripple flows along the line
and we are yesterdays, our highs and lows
recorded in old photographs. The fine,
the subtle arts we practiced no one knows.
The book is closed and gone the old design —
a part of history, a page of prose
or poetry. Yet words do not define
a life nor measure why the spirit chose
to honor, syncretize, or just decline.
A life encapsulated can't disclose.
A cone upon dry earth is not a pine.

*July 11-15, 2001*


ONCE MORE

I made a nest
in the chaos of beautiful old dust
rolling like a carpet
down the side of the bookcase
and curling along the baseboards
sheltering sow bugs.

Spiders hung their homes
in the corners and slid
silkily up and down,
sleeping when I slept
and waking only when
the light came up.

I was fragile as rain
breaking on the firs outside.

Days ticked by, 365 of them
to the countdown of the final second.
Silence clean as a knife
sliced through the past of shadows
and thrust me into the new year.

*Dec. 28 - Jan. 7, 1997*

## ONLY THE WIND

Lethargic the night rouses only with the wind.
From the nothing of long hours, exempt the wind.

The roof sings of the new cedar's fragrance,
its rich brown permeating only the wind.

Summer blooms with lithodora, hydrangeas,
tangling in blue combat against the wind.

July moves to its Olympiad races, sweaty,
euphoric, cacophonous, erasing the wind.

Dizzy with hope, athletes of the world
flex and reflect, damp fingers to the wind.

These voices that haunt the dark
twitch unclaimed. There is only the wind.

Going home, Old Lady, your final salute
is clocked by, borne on only the wind.

*July 28-29, 2012*


## A LITTLE ROUGHAGE

She hugs too close
so that bone and flesh
marry unwillingly.
Her strange austerity
seems not to warrant the act.
A planned demonstration of affection
is always suspect.

Yet perhaps she's under-read
with the glaze that time has laid across;
possibly her instincts baffled,
stifled by the press of years.
But drearily our culture whispers,
"Maybe she just wants to feel you up."

*Feb. 19-24, 2002*

## OLD MOTHER GOOSE

when she wanted to wander
took leave of her body
and that of the gander.

How glorious the universe
seen on her own –
the colors of language
murmured soft as the moss,
splintery as rain on wrinkle-dry earth,
chattery as hail on the bridge of her nose,
sibilant as sleep in a baby's repose.

What she had missed
was there all the time,
a simple uncoupling, outside of time,
of the mind from the body
to reason, to rhyme.

Old Mother Goose
when she wanted to wander
rode on the free way,
not on a gander.

*April 15, 2012*

## PIERCING THE MORTAL
(Regret for Hurtling Through the Classics)

Had my foresight been greater,
I would have made less of the adventure,
not been so hasty;
slowed for the substance
of those dark ancient words
though translated bone-thin.

I could have hugged into existence
the whole world of responses
and understood the reasons beneath
rather than just becoming vulnerable now
on the eve of my departure,
pierced through Achilles' heel.

*Jan. 29- Feb. 27, 2000*

## THE SPECTRUM

When red becomes orange,
the rainbow will fade.
When desire overcomes restraint,
the axe will sever.
When reason overrides compassion,
the heart will harden.

When grief becomes acceptance,
the calendar will keep time.

*April 19 - May 1, 2011; April 8, 2012*


## REVELATION AFTER DARK

I was so small
I could not speak.
I crept away,
afraid I'd break.

I learned too late
that silence split
in half
the whole of fate.

For now I dream
of other years,
the lives
I did not live;

of all those words,
unspoken then,
a thriving marsh
within my brain.

The clock ticks on.
My tongue stays tied,
and what I feel
I wear inside.

*Sept. 25-28, 2002*

## VALLEY WOMAN: LYIN' SKUNK

I cain't pull in m' horns.
I'm stayin' angered
at that Pinocchio in the White House
pickin' away at ever'thing decent
the law stands for;
playin' 'round with words,
insistin' that what wuz
don't matter if it ain't so now;
cheatin' on his wife
'n sayin' it don't count for nothin'
'cause it don't fit his definition o' sex
and that means he warn't lyin'.

I don't give a hoot 'bout the details
o' them li'l git-togethers
but I am fired up
over him tryin' to blind ever'body
with ever' trick in the books -
stallin'
'n duckin' ever' question ast him
even goin' so far as to git
two min'sters o' the Holy Word
to say he's a "broken man"
and truly repents.

What's he got to repent of?
He says he ain't done nothin' wrong.

*Dec. 2-6, 1998*


## POSSIBLY TEMPERATE

I am not yet warm.
I am not yet cold.

I cup one knee —
some heat to the touch,
but the hidden bone
is a knob of ice.
The difference divides me:
I am not yet warm.
I am not yet cold.

*April 8-11, 2009*

FINIALS

September in the north wind
wrinkles the flowers.
Like wet silk the blooms nose downward,
their stalks pointed south.
The hummingbirds feed on the fuchsia,
the frenzy of their wings contagious.

Summer battens down too soon.
The gloss is off the leaves.
The grass flattens.
Slugs are turgid,
draped openly across the darkened lobelia.

Quietly the garden dies.
Subtly the earth emits
the sweet scent of decay.
The haze of autumn pinkens at dusk.
Overnight on one last breath of warming wind,
a flotilla of dahlias  sways.

*Sept. 2-4, 1996*


INDECIPHERABLE

When I turned the corner
and came back,
you were someone else.

The dream became the reality,
the eruption of yesterday
startling the senses into agreement
but answering no questions,
the undiscovered remaining
the undiscovered.

Forever in the country of the blind
the mind sees
by tactile impressions
that the newborn snake
is only a worm.

*Feb. 5, 1997; Dec. 18, 2005*

## THE LAST DANCE

A whorl of dust, I shall dance unmarked
near wild blackberries and dandelion,
skimming over blossoming vetch
and pink clover.
Unaware, you'll sneeze me
like a pollen from your summer nose.

No sight of these old bones
swathed in their favorite purple,
no senseless wonder
at the yellowed cameo of this frozen face.

I shall enjoy my repose
unidentified,
the dance over,
my dust gently sifting onto living flowers.

*May 30 - June 5, 1996*


## INVOKING A TARDY SPRING

Bring out the bugles, the daffodil yellows,
sparaxis unequaled in orange display.
Burst open the azaleas, pop out the tulips.
I'm hungry for color to prick the gray day.

Brew up a sunshine, paint the sky blue.
Puff out some white clouds for birds to stream through.
I need contrast to feed me - color in hues.
Lithodora is all that I need of the blues.

*April 19, 2002*


## LAST NIGHT

the stars popped out in such staccato
the moon crescendoed through the window
usurping the bed.
There was so much noise
I retreated to the dark hall
leaving only my shadow in the doorway.

*Jan. 14-15, 2011*

239

## JANUARY MORNING

As frost fades
the sun reddens
making gold
the spiders' webs
strung through the trees.

The grass in blades
separated by rain
drags on my shoes.
I step away
head down,
alert for puddles,
their murkiness
bluing in the light.

Always wary
of the new year
I wilt under
its wet blanket
introduction.

The fringed yellow
of a lone dandelion
peers up at me.
And, morning springs
wide open.

*Jan. 2-11, 2009*


## TARGETS

The ant gliding over the sun-warmed rocks
does not feel the north wind
chilling the woman wedged in the corner,
twitching the fuchsia's  unleaved branches,
tattering the early bloom of the daffodil.
It is a matter of height, width, density—
the more space occupied,
the more likely the hit.

*March 12-15, 2009*

## THE MINED FIELD

Words on paper live, prickle —
their position giving emphasis.
Words spoken pierce, carry emotion
retained to haunt the years.

But for those who lie awake at night,
words effervescent,
bobble, swim, quiver —
phosphorescent in the flowing dark,
their life tenuous.
Neither written nor spoken
they die on the air
with the first flick of morning —
free of inflection, free of intent.

*Sept. 6 - Nov. 15, 2009*


## ONE-WAY STREET

Hey there, old lady
in your grandma shoes,
you can't go back
the way you came.
It's the law.
Once you're on this street
you have to keep the same direction.

The only way to go back
is to look over your shoulder
or like some folks
you can face around
to walk backwards.
You'll still be following
the rules but you'll
stumble, lose focus,
and be blind-sided by
whatever's coming to get you.

*June 7-13, 2009; April 18, 2010*

## VALLEY WOMAN: LONG DISTANCE

I been missin' my sister
since I heard she wuz in the hospital.

I called up her husband 'n told him,
"She always took care o' me."

"Um humm," he said.
"I knew that."

"You tell her, Bill," I said,
she's not to go poppin' off
before me "cause I need her
to hold my hand and show me the way
like she always did."

"Yes," he says.

He won't tell it to her like that
I know. He'll put it to her
in that soft min'ster's voice he's got
sose it won't sound nothin' like me
nor nothin' like I meant.
It'll be his message, not mine.

But, anyway, like he said,
I wuz the only one who called
and it'll warm her some
to know I did.

*Oct. 14-15, 1997*


## YEAR 2000

Nothing lasts forever
I foolishly believed;
but on the nineteenth anniversary
of your death, you had been gone
the same number of years you lived.

*July 31 - Aug. 1, 2000*

## AFTER THE RAIN

Just looking -
like water
running free of its banks
when its depth
exceeds its bounds;
stretching out,
filling the pockets first,
leveling the field.

I can wish to move like water
sinking into a parched earth,
saturating,
then flowing outward
investigating cedar groves,
earth-bound bulbs,
and the undiscovered country
where the gorse grows thick.

How little I would disturb,
how much I could discover,
freed from the narrow channel
I dig deeper every year.

*Nov. 26 - Dec. 2, 1996*


## SILENCE IS NOTHING

November spawns a lonely moon —
no clouds, no stars in the stretch of sky.
The night curls deeper to the shade of the house.
The street lies tight with sleep.

I listen, remembering the tardy hours
inching from second to minute
that year after year I waded through
anticipating your entrance.

But I wait no more — this continent away
The season has lost its power.
No turn of the knob, no click of the latch,
not even silence will open that door.

*Nov. 18-19, 2000*

THE BELL

"I'll ring the bell
to call you children home,"
my mama used to say.
Her way had always been
to ring the bell— not yell—
when our time was up
and home was where we were to be
beyond the clutch of dark.

Now two urns and a bell
lie beneath the swell of the Atlantic,
roped together
for what we think of as eternity.

Here, thousands of miles away,
someone repeatedly calls me out of sleep.
I wake,
my "yes" breathed into a silence
of the same world on which hours ago
I turned off the light.

But when the bell
that knows no continent or sea
sounds in my dream the lapse of time,
I'll wake to Mama welcoming me.

*Oct. 10-13, 2001*

*Note from my brother, Scott: "On August 11, 2001, at about 1:45 p.m., I put Mom's and Dad's ashes and the "cow" bell into the ocean about three-fourths of a mile off Pine Point in the Old Orchard Beach area in the state of Maine."*


UNCHARTED

A space only,
the afternoon nap
gulped time
wrapped around nothing.

*Jan. 9- 20, 2013*

## FOUR A.M. FEEDINGS

Years ago I was the four o'clock bird
of soft chirps, mothering in the dark
over the rustle of fledglings.

Night became my element.
I fed the nested,
rounding contours
and feathering in sleep.
Today would soon be yesterday;
none of this would matter.

Still I rouse at night
to cover what sleeps or lies awake,
accepting the penance for the past
to keep my faith in dreams intact.
For what is taught to slumber through the night
may wake larger than tomorrow's sun
and sear the known, the last horizon.

*June 3-11, 1997*


## THE DARK INSIDE

Madness does not grow. It is.
The mind wrinkled as worn silk
settles into quiet.
The acceptance,
cutting corners to the grave,
completes its little round.

Nothing is realized
walking on smoke shadows,
stumbling through sludge,
over dreams,
past hopes—
no fires to feed,
no blood thrumming,
only fear fluttering its tiny wings
at the naked edge of terror.

*June 25 - July 4, 1995*

245

## WHERE DO YOU GO ON CHRISTMAS MORNING?

"Could you help me out with a dollar?"
His was an open face
mottled pink  with the cold,
his eyes clear as sea water,
his clothes clean, color-matched.

"Merry Christmas," he had said
with a tentative smile
as I went into the only store open.

He was on that pale island
where we all have been
waiting for someone who would never come.
He could afford to size me up.
I gave him what he asked for.

All the day I damned
the society we have become
that I dared not question,
or linger, or look too closely.
I dared not move by heart.

*Dec. 26-28, 1998*


## JUNE DAYS

Chipping sparrows don't sing
yesterday's songs,
nor do Dachshunds
wriggling and yipping at morning.
The lithospernum reaches
farther each day
and weeds tuft into carpets.

Yesterdays are spent
with no final cadences
unless you number
your private worms.

*June 10-19, 1996*

# A REED, A THINKING REED

Impulsively,
hands over her face,
she rolled down the steep incline
into the gully of the wild ferns.
Deep in the green scent
of the living and the dead,
she curled tight.

The sun needled warmth
through the firs;
birds thumped their wings
in startled flight over her head.
She cradled her cheek on one arm.

"I shall go to earth here,
looking out yesterday's window;
sop up the elements
until my flesh melts.
My bones will bleach
and be no more than a bridge
across the landscape
for birds and insects."

The image rattled like a dry frond.
Thought would be silenced
by wind swoops,
crows' gutturals,
insect tickings.
Clouds would grow spongy
feathering into blue.
The light would come and go
and the dark torment her
like a rough blanket.

Scrunching on all fours,
the twilight narrowing her vision,
she measured the distance upward
and clawed her way out.

*July 24 - Aug.6, 1996*

## VALLEY WOMAN: CIRCUS TRAIN

I been haulin' this circus train o' mis'ry
ever since I borrowed from yesterday.
Ever' one of them cars holds some wild thing
never been subdued by its envir'nment
and not even the littlest bit tamed by time passin'.

If I could, I'd pull this ole train on a sidin',
git myself out 'n peer in them cages
sose I could size up whatall was in there
and take 'em on, one at a time,
startin' with the smallest.

I betcha that once I got to rasslin'
on an individual basis,
and come to that last cage,
bustin' it wide open,
I wouldn't find nothin' but one big shadow
that'd melt down 'fore I ever got my arms 'round it.

*Nov. 3-12, 1997*


## DECEMBER DITTY

You are not as you were
the mirror confirms —
the brown drained from your hair,
the lines drooped on your face.

You taste this wry salt
with the tip of your tongue;
know the bubbles have burst,
the rainbows are gone.

You follow a pattern
turned into a maze
where corners are rounded
and streets a zigzag.

Yet you open the boxes
you've opened before.
Christmas lies waiting
to resurrect joy.

*Dec. 6-14, 2002*

## OBSOLETE FACES

The little boy looked worried.
"Do you know what time it is?"

"Ten minutes 'til eleven."

Puzzled, he asked,
"Does that mean ten-fifty?"

How I dwindled in that frame of reference
with the memory of Big Ben, Baby Ben,
and Seth Thomas faces before me,
of the soft tick-tocks
and sometimes loud ones
that needed muffling,
of the nightly ritual of winding
"not too much; you'll break it,"
of watching the minute hand
slide
slide
slide
moving time along
toward the quarter-after,
the half-past,
the quarter-of,
and finally the hour.

How those hands fingered away the days.
No reason to be a clock-watcher now —
there's nothing to see.

*Feb. 16-18, 1998*


## A GOOD POEM

A good poem is a pinch of pepper
without the sneeze —
the distending of the nares
and the intake of breath
just before the heart stops.

*Feb. 16 - 17, 2002*

GARDEN VARIETY 1

After a long time
I dream my way into the garden.
The blue fairy materializes
above the scent of roses
over the clusters of lilac
far from the damp cool of earth.
With cupped hands
she eases flowers
from the pregnant air,
the silence lush,
joy undulating
in color and form.

Below, in revel,
the ground-huggers, earthbound,
keep their integrity of substance and fragrance.
Illusions evaporate.

*Feb. 19-23, 2008*


GARDEN VARIETY 2

So, Miss Rose,
you want to be a jonquil,
shout spring from your mouthy trumpet,
grace the church altars at Easter?

May I warn you that you will carry no sweet fragrance,
that as you age you will dry and crinkle on your stem,
and there will be no soft sloughing
petal by petal into oblivion.

*Feb. 21-23, 2008*

## THE BACK YARD

I have begun to live
behind the house
with the woodpile
artfully constructed and tarped
now slithering out to rot;
the terrace
where I had zinnias, herbs, and wallflowers
caved in by rain and dogs.

Here I feel at home with my slow uncoupling —
a consciousness of tremor,
the weight of blood and bone and tissue,
fuzziness of vision,
narrowing breath,
and ears attuned to silence
ringing with an unfamiliar song.

*June 30 - July 10, 2005*


## THE SKY'S THE SAME

These are the short hours when you wake listening
for the one-two syllable ticks of a clock that no longer exists —
the luminous digital harsh with a reality you're forced to confront:
Nothing has a familiar face.

You remember being clamped in your seat
slipping over the top of the Ferris wheel,
your stomach, breath, and sense of direction struggling to catch up,
the dark space around you prickling.
Then the glorious shock inhaled, more than breath,
the stun of color, movement, and sound—
anachronistic, disparate, unsettling as you descend,
unhook the bar, and step off.

*Nov. 24-30, 2008*

GOING HOME

I am nearing that green field
I've never seen but know is there,
bordered with wild rhododendron,
wild fuchsia and the cedar tree
with its crisp scent apparent
only if I nose in close enough.
Directionless, I have been on my way
for decades, somehow sensing
regardless of the circuitous route,
the destination will not change.

*June 28 - July 4, 2008*


A WAY OUT

She read it again:
"Picasso to be in Los Angeles,"
delight arresting her mouth
in a soft line.

"It's the right time.
"I can go home now."

Her luggage matched to a traveling suit,
she boarded the bus,
putting aside the blank face
of Alaska she had known
only from her hotel window;
pushing away those alien days
spent cramped in the restaurant corner;
and the nights when,
rigid with terror in the massive bed,
she had listened wide-eyed
to the thumps in the hall.

"I have a place with yellow curtains,
an alcove of sunshine,
and plants I have nurtured,
a table with two chairs—
one for company—
and Picasso to meet at the museum."

*Oct. 22-26, 1996*

## THE CIRCLE

Something is always lurking
five times bigger than you,
prepared to pounce
should you fail to guard.

The hunter and the hunted,
forever the same.

Behind the walls
the mice keep asking,
"Who will bell the cat?"

No one ever answers.

*April 10-14, 2006*


## THE TELEPHONE

At the tone the time will be
not for me, not for me.
At dawn and dark the moon will eye
the sun somewhere between.
The light, the gracious sifting screen
between the tides' and seasons' change,
is no boxed voice that hoarsely claims
time will be, time will be.

Time is space, a monotone
between goodbye, hello;
a curiously unmeasured beat
awake, asleep, awake, asleep.

*Oct. 26, 1983; Sept. - Oct. 2011*


## FOUR SCORE AND MORE

I wish to angle sharp
in the muscle-taut semblance of youth,
but only the strength of the reed is in me now
softening, bending and buckling,
the reed that thinks to keep from breaking.

*Feb. 6-14, 2010*

## VALLEY WOMAN:  COMIN' UNSTUFFED

I'm comin' all unstuffed
like my ole blue-star quilt,
insides driftin' on the wind
in a sorta horizontal free fall.

They's no shape left to me.
I done give up tryin'
to plump myself up
for this person or that
or ev'ry show'r or party goin".

Yessir, I'm tellin' the world
that this ole girl thinks
it's pretty much all over
until the Hallelujah Chorus.

*Oct. 29, 1997*


## EYES WIDE OPEN

Raggedy Ann,
I'm weary of this mimicry.
All night I face the ceiling, button-eyed,
my body limp and floppy,
the batting in my head clumped.
It's time to cut the threads,
plump up with new stuffing,
wear grown-up clothes,
and clear the eyes.
I would however like a final ride
on your friendly paper dragon.
I've fought so many in disguise.

*Jan. 30 - Feb. 1, 2008*


## JANUARY 1, 2007

Take a small black dog outside at night
to learn that shadows have substance.
It is impossible to tell which is which.
Lacking vision, a lie can be truth in disguise.

## LITTLE SEAS

"I would not go again," she wrote.
Then I knew she too had floundered,
her story not the same as mine
but yet how slim the difference —
the same long odds,
short sight, rich dreams,
and waking late with graying hair
to how small we used to be.

*April 15-18, 2001*


## LITTLE PRONOUNCEMENTS

Privacy is self-made,
but bounds can be burst.
Stand back from what invades.
Learn intentions first.

What can break I face.
What will keep I lose.
What will stay, unknown.
Hold nothing close.

There is life, there is death,
each scarcely a flutter:
storm and a calm —
the center of one, the other.

*Aug. 24-31, 2003*


## DEM DRY BONES

Little of tomorrow is left for these bones —
to channel pain and cold into dreams,
to pulverize intellect into idiocy,
to give shape to the flesh in its wrinkled sleep
before the final flame reduces them to dust.

And, then —
they will fly with the wind.

*June 22-29, 2006*

## THE COMPUTER

Its dark face reflects me
and the room behind
with its three open doors,
the outer world
muted, suggesting
egress and ingress.

Its pressed button brings
light to yesterday's
unfinished files,
resurrecting
a temporary oblivion.

*May 20 - June 2, 2012*


## MERE WORDS

Nothing more than words
stings
flays
scars.
Under the skin whole alphabets
contrive
writhe
burrow
vying for ascendancy
from red
to purple
to black.

Words are what you use
when actions aren't.
Words are what you fill space with
when silence won't.

Mere words.

*March 16-20, 2004*

## VALLEY WOMAN: OLE FRIEND

"You jest pourin' shadows in my cup,
Lucy," I says. "I don't want that.
It's too much doomsayin'.
You tellin' me hark the heralds sing
disaster. It don't help me none
to stand there tremblin',
tryin' to guess how deep the water is
'fore I get tipped in."

"Givmme soma that tea's
been settin' there steamin.'
It'll go down black 'n savage
smackin' up against my gut
sose I'll know from the hot pain
I can still feel somethin' in this  world.

*Aug. 27, 1997*


## HOLDING OFF

Some little thing
from some little day
will rise like dust to fill your eyes.

It's better the second time around they say.

But you know
the little thing from that little day
will fret like a healing scab.

*April 10-14, 2006*


## ERASURES

I'm giving you forgetfulness, he said.
He was right —
ravaged by consent, signing the paper
for the raw throat, the slashed flesh,
and no memory of infliction.

*2007*

## AFTER ONE HUNDRED YEARS

I take you from your suitcase, Margarita Angeline,
your hair frowsy from long sleep.
I'm drawn to you, knowing you were loved,
and to your first owner, moving gracefully
just beyond my physical reach,
who was loved even more.

On these mornings the grass stilled, icy,
the sky sullenly gray, uncompromising,
I need you, Margarita Angeline,
need to do what Mama said,
"Pick her up and hold her sometimes."
Or, did she say "love her"? No matter.
They are the same —to have and to hold.

You are no stranger to this cuddling.
Despite your stiffness, you tuck comfortably in my arms,
born to it, defined by it, revived by it.

I touch your blushed china cheeks,
look into your blue eyes
(not quite Mama's forget-me-not blue),
wince at that tight leather bodice,
smooth the petticoat layers.
finger the delicate crochet on the bloomers,
ease up the gauzy socks drooping over the blue shoes.
We rock, serene together, unclocked.

For now, I will enclose you
where you can be best protected
from fade, mold, and dust.
Love can do that.

*Feb. 8-18, 2013*


## COMFORT

I cannot fashion much for you,
you strange neglected child.
But when the streets go black with rain,
the monster rears from shadowed haunts,
and fear usurps your trembling limbs,
I can make a little mother of the dark.

*Nov. 16-26, 2002*

258

## VALLEY WOMAN: GIVE WHATCHA GOT

Sittin' here drinkin' this tea
I get to thinkin'
maybe I been steeped too long
'n what's left o' me
ain't fit for man or beast.

That kinda thinkin' brings to mind
somethin' someone once tol' me
'bout Ann Frank in the concentration camp.
She had an ol' tea bag
that she swirled 'round in a cup o' water
to give to someone comin' in new.

It was what she had to offer.

*Feb. 23-27, 2000*

## SENSING JUNE

In the grass
the wind's voice
is green; its face
indiscernible.

In the air a trill,
the bird's lone call
blue as an oyster shell
dried in the sun.

On the ground
the slug and worm brown,
a smear and a wiggle unsung
in this craze of sounds.

*June 2-3, 2012*

## OUTSIDE THE BOX
(Not All Skies Are Blue)

What is the color for old?
No, not that one.
That one is for a certain anniversary,
a gloriously prolific era,
an opportunity for the wary or unwary,
a parachute,
a calf.

Old is yellow.
The teeth, the hair, the skin, whites of the eyes
dwindle to it
as do leaves, fronds, and flower petals.
It is the color that goes to earth most easily —
celebratory.

*Feb. 27-28, 2009*




## THE DEVIL YOU SAY

Be the Devil's advocate?
Outrageous that he should seek me out.

If too angered by his insistence,
I am in his clutch.
If moved to pity or charity,
I am in his pocket,
grouped with the amoral—
sensual and insensate.

He has no case.
It would be thrown out of court.
Interview denied.

*Oct. 25-26, 2001*

## HAIKU OF 1998

Buffeted by time
I wear the season winter
but not in my heart.

Beneath the willow
I learned to hide from myself
when the wind was still.

*Feb. 14, 1998*

## NIPPED IN THE BUD

Something else was waiting
in the cool gray dawn.
Something else was watching
for the sepals to curve down
and the coral petals loosen
on the last rose of summer.

"I'll delay no longer,"
I thought in all my ignorance.
"Tomorrow I'll clip the promise
and a rose will bloom at dinner."

At 9 A.M. scissor-handed
I crossed the beaded grass,
anticipating pleasure
reveling in the flower.

But something had come earlier,
more cognizant of time.
The stem stood starkly naked;
the last bud of summer gone.

*Dec. 11, 1996*

## WIND CHIMES

They hang there, wooden,
their melodies lost in hollows
of once living trees.

The wind, coming in gentle waves,
soothes their planed edges,
nudging them to touch
and in touching express themselves —
a burbling keen —
so that being carved singly
need not keep them separate,
need not keep them mute.

*Nov. 26, 2011; July 14-17, 2012*


## MEASURES

She sang in a house that never accepted her.
The songs piled up in the closet, hoarse with dust,
the words no longer distinguishable.
One night the melodies escaped,
floating raggedly through her sleep
like old lace drifting from a flannel gown.
She knew crescendo and diminuendo.
In the gray dawn, unencumbered, she disappeared.

*July 5-22, 2007*


## ONSLAUGHTS

Loopy with November rain splopping on my window,
the outside of me betraying the inside with a crooked smile,
I tasted the wind, letting the sand and salt explode on my tongue;
then spat out those fragments of my universe.

It is what I've always done — taken a taste here, spat there,
yet somehow absorbed enough to seam, pit, and channel myself
into a landscape I verify.

*Nov. 9-16, 1999*

## THE OBSERVATORY

Yesterday,
bare-boned
I walked
past naked windows
appraising me.

Today,
mere pounds of flesh
I lurch past.
The windows
drop their blinds.
But, through the slats
I see one dark eye
wink at me.

*May 19-22, 2011*


## THINKING OUTSIDE

Come out of the box
red, green, and silver,
tinsel and manger,
white-booted Santa.

Away dust and ashes.
Away cockle-burr heart.
The season's unwrapping;
I must have a part.

Come out of the box
and drain me of time.
The moon is the same
viewed with new eyes.

No beach is too barren,
stones can be turned,
a flicker of starlight
become the whole sky.

*Dec. 5, 2000; Feb. 19, 2011*

## VALLEY WOMAN: HARVEST

All them plants sittin' out there,
they's mostly geraniums,
reds, pinks, and the fluffy purple one on the end.

I bought 'em over the years
and set 'em in my narrow porch
sose sometimes I could purely drown in color.
They's only a glass door between us.

Mornin's when I'm drinkin' my tea and lookin' out,
I get to smilin' 'bout what I paid for happiness.
Oh, some of it was at the reg'lar price
but mostly it was bargain-rate.

*July 20-29, 1997*


## BEDDING DOWN

Early
the mint scent of October,
the slug gorging on the impatiens,
a spider webbing its dinner,
sparrows flurrying through the hedge
to gobble meaty worms.

Not bare, not yet brown.
One pink-edged rose,
the fuchsia's delicate ballerina blossoms
suspended in quiet,
the grass sleepy with dew
and the sky coming up mauve from the ocean.

Time to leave damp footprints on the walk,
repot the geraniums,
to bury dead hopes
and mulch spring dreams
locked in bulbs and sleeping seeds.

Time to go dormant
beneath the scatterings of summer,
to be nurtured,
fed strength,
to know winter as only muffled thunder
above the mothering earth.

# EVERY WITCH WAY

The midnight face of the clock:
What was seen as fixed in daylight hours
looses its hold and moves about.
The elm that shaded the garden gate
shivers and whispers against the house.
The stones that traced the flower beds
zigzag and disappear in space.
The hydrangea's clump and the lily's cup
have lost the stems that thrust them up.
And what of my feet that knew the way
now angled and sliding like wayward ships
that have no compass or star?

The clock strikes again
and the hour is gone
every witch way but one.

*June 14-15, 1999*


# CONNECTIONS

The letters came
from Charlie in Maryland "I think she died peacefully,"
from Lois In Ohio "It was all downhill after that,"
from Marilyn in West Virginia "Fifty-three years of being loved."

Each time a great knock in my chest,
prelude to resurrections defining a lifetime
half a century ago.

Susan, a warm jewel once given that proper setting;
Jerry, who treated Lois like a piece of fine china;
Sam, loving laughter and humanity but most of all Marilyn.

These are my lifelines.

*Jan. 15-20, 2007*

## STRIKING THE COLORS

I had not known
that colors mourn
their lost identity,
but I learned.

Purple sickens
with too much yellow.

Red howls
when orange overwhelms.

Yellow shrieks
overdosed with green.

Blue chafes
inundated by purple.

Black oblivious to inconstancy
greedily swallows them all.

*June 22 - July 26, 2010*


## GOING OUT

I am forever growing old,
trimming the level of exposure
to a bare nubbin,
everything that is, isn't,
everything that was, is,
letting the dark ease up warm and comforting
and my last sputters be forgotten as my first.

Am I merely waiting to gutter out
like a candle into its own melted flesh?

*Dec. 14-21, 1997*

## VALLEY WOMAN: LISTEN UP

You listen up!
It's time to undream yourself,
stop shufflin' your past
like you was playin' solitaire
lookin' for matchin' cards.

I tell you, Gal,
there's no sense you lookin' for answers.
Once you get old, ever'thing's all muddled up.
You git so you caint remember
if you lived it or dreamed it.

You outside ever'thing
like the world done divorced you
and slammed the door in your face.
It's kinda like bein' the frame
'round the pitchur the sun shone on fifty years
sose it's all light and dark shadows,
could be anythang or nothin'.

How you gonna make sumpin outta that?

*June 25, 1997*



## A DITTY FOR NOW AND THEN

Now is the time, when rain is slight,
to skim the grasses, reflect the light
until no heaviness remains
and regret has gone to earth.

Then is the time when torrents rain,
flattening the grasses, blotting the light
until only heaviness can sit
a frozen stone upon the heart.

No thens or nows but in-betweens
give balance to the months and years.
Dark and light flip off and on,
the current intermittent.

*June 3, 2006; Dec. 8-9, 2007*

MORE THAN MUSIC
(For Michael Smith)

Michael's music swells undammed,
drenching the senses
until the heart, exposed,
picks up the beat.

Everything stored breaks open again;
but softly
as a warm river surrounding,
defining you,
lifts you up, one small island,
its link to the mainland obscured.

*Feb. 2-13, 1999*


NO LESS A THING THAN MEMORY KEEPS ME STRONG

No less a thing than memory keeps me strong.
It's harbored in my blood. I know its grace.
No arbiter determines right or wrong.

The unresolved no longer flood my heart.
The dark imperfect years have left no trace.
No less a thing than memory keeps me strong.

No act or thought becomes a studied art
to agitate my brain, reshape my face.
No arbiter determines right or wrong.

This wealth, this rainbowed gift,  can still impart
the warmth of flowers delicate as lace.
No less a thing than memory keeps me strong.

I have no wish to make another start,
to force my thoughts into a foreign place.
No arbiter determines right or wrong.

The hour, the time replete, I shall depart
with these intangibles that I embrace.
No less a thing than memory keeps me strong.
No arbiter determines right or wrong.

*Nov. 27- Dec. 15, 2000*

## POST- SURGERY: MAJOR INSULT

When the littles become big,
all borders disappear.

Stepping out is stepping in,
into foreign territory, prickling a sense
that you once walked there in some forgotten childhood
exultant at the strength of the wind,
the intense light from the sky,
the pebbly crunch of earth.

Your feet are newly hewn,
moving toddler fashion, certain yet uncertain,
the movement consuming you
forcing a rational acceptance
that what has seemingly changed has not.

*Dec. 29, 2010 – Jan. 1, 2011*


## THE WORD PIT

I hear them in their nakedness
coupling and uncoupling
sighing and groaning
gasping and moaning
giggling and murmuring
changing partners
in an orgy of procreation.

I ease into their cloistered space
seeking conjugation
but there are only disintegrates—
an alphabet of black roundings,
arcs and stick-straight lines –
their passion spent,
inaccessible.

*Jan. 25-30 , 2011*

ECLIPSES

Who can tire of the nattering crow,
the windless break that prinks the flowers,
the gust of clouds that pale the sun,
the startle of the sudden rain?

Who can turn from ragging grief,
be like the tree whose branches know
just when to release the exhausted leaves
and gather strength in dormancy?

Can it be I who does not tire,
who knows to turn as seasons do;
that what is lost is only hidden
in another time, a different form?

*Oct. 19-21, 2001*


AT THE VISITATION

"You look more like your mother than any of the other girls."

My mother, fair, slender, well-proportioned.
I, squat and dark.
I smiled respectfully.

"There it is," they said.

What I had not known before warmed me.
My mother had left me her smile,

*Oct. 25-26, 1994*


ADVENT

Little Mary, age thirteen, asks
How can it be? Why me?

Too young to know
these are always the questions.

*.Dec. 7-11, 2009*

VALUES

Perhaps it does not matter after all.
She stirs her tea, the sugar swirling up.
      The flowers flaunt their colors in salute.
      The hedge of escallonia shelters birds.
She stirs her cooling tea and  takes one sip.
      Things are as they've always been, inner-lit.

*Dec. 5- 7, 2008*


IF NOT THE SWORD, THE PLOWSHARE

Autumn seems suspended by a thread.
Uneasy lies the head, pillowed or not,
the ears tuned for the spirited gusts,
the eyes alert for weeds hurried to bed.

Suddenly the rain strikes,
ringing like minute coins against the glass,
smashing the face of summer.
Whether early or late
there's no retrieving of moment.

*Oct. 30-31, 2010*


LESS THAN PERFECT

I follow the Dachshund path
through the grass, past the trees,
to where the dew lies in crystals
under the unbroken sun.

Armed with a trowel, I hunt
for the replica, the lesser sun,
the dandelion.

Always the imitation engages the eye,
fascinating but failing in comparison,
justifying the uprooting.

*May 1-2, 2011*

## CIRCLING THE SPACE

I filled a bowl with bright apples
to light up the emptiness,
to make sense of loss.
It required more:
Whole libraries of compilations,
volumes disinterred,
to be taken up singly and examined.

But nothing fills the space you left.
There are only evocative yesterdays,
elusive as the wind
that suddenly slips through a chink
and surprises the eyes to tears.

*Dec. 21-29, 1994*


## AUTUMNAL EQUINOX

Forlorn
under the lean sun
the calendulas glow
yellow
against the dead spaces
of last week's tigridia.

Leaves thin,
branches harden.
A lone grasshopper
turgidly leaps
upon my shoe
and despairingly plunks
into the straggle of lobelia.

Fog sifts
onto the unformed glads.
A mauve sunset
deepens the blue of the hyacinth,
resurrects the blood red of the roses.

Night shrouds,
erasing all trace of color.
Only the white moon blooms.

*Sept. 22 - Oct. 5, 1993*

## THE SIXTH DECADE

Sleep blurs
the contrived harmony
of bed with body.
You rise, muddled still,
stained with dreams.

Not exactly foot-in-mouth,
ear-to-the-ground,
or shoulder-to-the-wheel
disparities plague you,
but a certain
unhinged decision
on how to walk,
see,
hear,
get a bearing
in the newborn universe.

Mornings used to be simple:
One quick swing
of legs to the floor,
a fluid elevation of torso,
and the mind snapped to,
the order of the day
inviolate.
Now it is
where,
how,
and who are you?

Yesterday has gone down
like a tipped domino trail.
Clutter-headed,
you climb from debris
and take direction
from external stimuli,
the clock,
doorbell,
telephone scream.

Time ticks
a second late.
Lucidity has sunk
below the horizon,
as lost as last year's sunset.

*Jan. 4-15, 1996*

## NOT ABOUT TIME

The calendar keeps no time:
Monday for two days
and twenty years a yesterday.

Light always stretches to fill the sky,
the low hills hunker purple,
flowers support the spiders' hammocks,
and the brown earth prickles.

With both decay and promise I endure,
clocked by the hello of morning:
No death has ever been goodbye.

*July 30 - Aug.4, 2001*


## GOING TO SLEEP

Erasing the wind whispers at the door,
the leaves' conversation outside the window,
the faint evergreen scent sifting down the hall,
the moon's glaze on the ceiling,
to fall softly into a universe of silence
and drift endlessly with my old ghosts.

*Dec. 14-16, 1997*


## LOOKING OUT THE WINDOW

I remind myself
that the print I leave
on the frosted glass
will change shape
as the ice melts,
as the sun inches
warmth through the pane.

Some semblance of my hand
may linger, a smear
against clear sky.
The housekeeper
will polish it away.

*May 5-7, 2004*

# THE HOLLOW HOUSE

Sounds slap against the walls,
returning uninflected,
flat and alien against her ears.

A pale sun seeks
the missing bookcase,
the red-eyed clock.

Bare walls hold the impressions
of vanished pictures.

A thin dust hugs the windowsill
behind the phantom leather chair.

Silence stretches to its breaking point.
She cannot find a voice.

*Feb. 23 - March 6, 2012*


# VALLEY WOMAN: KALEIDOSCOPE

I keep gettin' visits from yesterd'y
poppin' up to surprise me,
like unexpected guests
that get you all a-twitter,
skippin' 'round tryin' to 'commodate 'em.

Nobody ever tol' me
I'd go all mushy in the head
livin' a double life,
the one I already had
'n the one I'm tryin' to have now.

When I put my mind to it,
it's like I'm a child again
lookin' in a kaleidoscope,
the pieces all loose then comin' together
to make a whole diff'rent world.

*April 19-22, 1999*

## AFTER SEPTEMBER 11, 2001

The dark breeds light illuminating fear.
In isolation fright constructs a frame.
The wits cease wandering. The haze burns clear.

For out of ash the phoenix will appear
a gloat of wings, a resurrection claim.
The dark breeds light. Illuminating fear

reveals the enemy in sharp contour
and quickens sense, ignites the blood to tame
the wits.  Cease wandering: The haze burns clear.

The residue is sifted. Towers veer,
indomitable emblems that proclaim
the dark breeds light, illuminating. Fear

gives rise to power, kindles courage, tier
on tier above the ravaged site. Shame
the wits. Cease wandering. The haze burns clear.

These acts have stripped us of our thin veneer,
superiority. We're all the same.
The dark breeds light, illuminating fear.
The wits cease wandering; the haze burns clear.

*Dec. 17-27, 2001;  Jan. 6, 2002*


## ACHIEVEMENT

I learned to erase facial expression
so that I could not be read,
to lower my eyelids if doubtful.
I became so proficient that nothing betrayed me.
I could join a group and never be acknowledged.
I was the space in a crowd.
When I no longer required even that,
I simply evaporated.

*Jan. 12-26; Feb. 24, 2006*

## SAME OLD, SAME OLD

The wind plays old tunes
to the quarter moon
that refuses to be wooed.
Its crescent mouth of cream,
betraying nothing
of the human incursion
that bounced on its surface,
maintains its sidewise smile
oblique and seductive.

*May 7-8, 2011*


## CIRCLING THE SPHERE

Too long dazed with sun
and sodden with the hot moon,
I stretched toward October
in the twittering heart of the woods.
Feathers fell and small seed pods
wisped through the air.

Only a whisper
but it is coming.
The sun will melt down,
the moon whiten,
and bare trees stiffen
against the advancing wind.

Only a nudge
and I will remember the inherent power
in powerlessness; that the season's
sloughing of leftovers, wornouts, unsuitables
dapples the ground with texture and color,
that it crunches underfoot,
and melds,
and is the sustenance for sproutings
after the winter's gestation

*Sept. 14 - Oct. 1, 1995*

## VALLEY WOMAN: LIVIN' OUTSIDE

My mind's  churnin' up so much dust these mornin's
it's been takin'  more than tea to unmuddle me.

There's a whole yardful o' things
poppin' up glad to be alive,
soakin' in God's sunshine and rain.

Be nice to think I could put out new leaves
'n bud inta flow'rs
so's anyone lookin' could say
"There's a sight for sore eyes"
without payin' no mind
to the dried-up ol' stick that produced 'em.

*April 7-12, 1999*


## TO AND FRO

The book I wanted was on the now-empty shelf.
I extended my hand for its shabby cover,
its title, its author I no longer knew.

Foggy mornings sprout these ancients.
I am singing soundlessly
of the cannibal king with the big nose ring
who fell in love with a dusky maid
and every night it sounded.

(Up and down it goes
and where it stops no one knows.)

I cannot find my dying place.
Perhaps that is a given grace
to keep me upright, mobile.

*Sept. 8-10, 2012*

## PRE-DAWN

These bitter draughts I swallow humbly
have not and cannot make me free
of worms' desire.

My service, cups of latent fire
that gulped down feed my funeral pyre,
tarnishes ultraviolet.

Flakes of ashes faintly sweet
choke the narrowing well and cheat
my thirsty tongue.

Broken are my days, unsung,
and sharp the hourless night that's strung
with stubborn reason.

Here and now is the only season
left to salt my weary run.
Out of dust I speak.

*April 14, 1993*


## IN LEFT FIELD

Who knows my name I do not know.
By wandering in the dark, I sense
those others  seeking how to go
as I, as we, as all do so —nameless.

Uncharted, stumbling or assured,
we seek our place, our entity,
but lose it all with the toll of years
and learn how comforting it is.

*Dec. 18-30, 2012*

## COUNTING OUT

One two I'm going through
three four an unlocked door
five six nothing conflicts
seven eight I may be late
nine ten I can't say when
eleven twelve I'll resolve
thirteen fourteen how I've been
fifteen sixteen what I mean
seventeen eighteen clear the screen
nineteen twenty my place empty.

*1992, Fall; Oct. 26-29, 2004*


## AN OLD WOMAN IN LEAP YEAR

The old woman knows the moon,
has seen its secrets spill from the clouds
unexpectedly in startling illumination;
knows the sun too and how to sop up its warmth
despite the wind's chill, leaning her hobbled body
against the  south side of the house;
knows the surprise of snow in April
sliding off the blooming tulips,
heightening the humbled color
of the masses of wild violets;
knows without having seen
that in the desert, Anza Borrego,
flowers bloom every spring.

*March 7 - April 20, 2008*

## EVOLUTIONS

In June one learns the beauty of spent things:
Wind-loosed cherry blossoms kissing the street,
the dead tree branch half-hidden in the undergrowth,
its twiggy fingers glistening in the fog,
the brown stench of rotted leaves
mixing with the green of freshly cut grass.

Every year it is the same, new to the senses,
these small fragments gathered, formed into a pattern,
and filed under inevitable.

*May 24 - July 29, 2007*

## A STAY OF COURAGE

I winter in this lapse
of April, shadowless
under the pearl gray;
soaking up nutrients
distilled from the past,
refusing to be vulnerable.

But the swallows rustle,
tacking nests in the eaves;
frogs blare
in pure cacophony;
the moon rises
new in a freshening sky;
and the dark breeds
the scent of flowers.

*April 4-18, 1994*

## BEEN THERE, NOT DONE THAT

I've been there
but for all the good it did me
I might well not have,
with personalities and egos
flowing over me
in a drowning sea.

I've merely grown smaller
until only I can see myself
filling the empty chair –
and that in retrospect.

So I scribble in my narrow words
pinched as I am pinched,
phrasing myself in concentric circles
with no beginning, no end,
no entrance, no exit.

*Aug. 3-4, 2000*


## HOW

How shall I marvel
when no breath of spring
turns January to April,
when deep in color
the primrose purses from earth,
a time-wrenched iris
opens white petals to rain,
and a single Lithodora blinks blue?

In this frostless excuse for winter,
how shall I not?

*Jan. 2-3, 1996*

FAUX-NAIF

No apocalypse
of stunned eyes
shrieking mouth
collapsing knees,
only one swift glance
of recognition:
Death.

*May 11-13, 2012*


GARDENS

In the night I flittered
through shards of rainbows.
They were soft, not brittle,
a curious insubstantial
like colored air
or reflections on water.

I gathered armfuls
of old dreams,
grown large as peonies
with no more life or fragrance than wax.

A gray wind
screaming under the eaves
woke me.
On tiptoe I leaned out
and saw the daffodils fight
to keep a footing
in the damp earth
and the newborn mauve tulips
like small fists
beat furiously
against the invisible enemy.

*March 17-19, 1997*

## BACK STAGE WITH A LEPRECHAUN

"Hello," he said,
popping his head between the curtains.
"This is an old building I can tell;
I'm a builder."

He paused, gesturing.
"There's storage area over there, right?
"Maybe more back there?"

I nodded and responded,
"I keep hearing someone there."

"Ssh," he said, forefinger to lips,
head cocked to the right for five seconds.
"It's a little girl."

Moving on soft feet to the ladder,
he listened again.
"Where are you, honey?"

He pointed.
"I think she's up there."

"It's locked. I'll try the other side.
"Do they connect? No?"

He swung up by his hands,
legs springing wide from the ladder.
"Not here."

He came then to center stage.
"My wife gets angry," he said,
"thinks I sound crazy.
"It's all out there I tell her.
"You just don't notice."

*April 24, 1996*

X-RAYED

You are looking into a tomb.
It has nothing to do with skin or blood,
ligaments or tendons,
nor with ears or nose,
hair, or the shape of the face.

What you see is only a decaying landscape
with dirty patches of snow
bisected by a highway of tire tracks.

You prickle:
Inside, you are black and white and cloudy
and, outside, your eyes and brain do not synchronize.
You never get the whole picture.

*Nov. 29 – Dec. 2, 2007*


THE REQUEST

Give me yesterday:
the hour, the minute, rush, sway,
halt of heart on the half-beat;
three-quarters at least of the sun
and the vast sweep of the wind
billowing sails of dust;
scraps of dahlia and rose
petaling the ground;
the yellow slug on the mums,
moist leap of grasshoppers,
the roar and scent of the fishsweet sea,
evening queries of birds;
and one full moon
pouring a snow on the weathered deck.
Then I shall be who I was.

*Oct. 14, 1993*

BEING RAW

It is the time to be small,
hide under a down quilt
where the curtains
barely register the movement
to shadow the ceiling and walls.

It is best to be unseen,
to quell one's storms alone
when your sister leaves without you.

*Sept. 3-17, 2012*


A LETTER

Dear World,
I write this to you
by the beat of my blood
flowing to my fingers
clenched on a ball-point pen.

Scoop up my words
and let your tongue
feel the shapes
of the letters
before the mind accepts
the sense.

You will give me joy
more holy than not,
softening the edges of my fixed island
into a burgeoning sea.

*Aug. 3-4, 1999*

CERBERUS

Orpheus
facing the sting of hell
startled at the sight of Cerberus,
not the three heads
nor the dragon tail
but the obvious stump
of a missing leg.

Pity sprouted
in his careful heart.
He lowered the range
of his golden notes
in deference to
those sensitive ears;
and passing through
that den of frantic souls
made of hell
a little heaven.

That lapse of purpose,
compassion over deed,
betraying him,
he turned too soon,
arms open to Eurydice
who sinking back
with a hollowed whisper of "Farewell"
was echoed by the frosty knell
of Cerberus chained forever
at the gates of hell.

*Aug. 29 - Sept. 3, 2000*


IN THE OFFING

When old houses begin to creak,
old ladies must keep their reason
or succumb to childhood fantasy
and magnify the source

Old bats and bats in the belfry
are similar yet distinct.
Since I'm one, I have the other
but I may not know it yet.

*Dec. 15-16, 2012*

287

## ADAPTING

As I move, clumsily now,
through the woods netted in mist,
into the unexplored world of old age,
I learn the intrinsic value of each of my limbs,
the torso dependent on their functioning,
remember how Yeats questioning his condition
asked what he should do with
"this caricature, decrepit age."

I laugh as I note my walk has grown similar
to the crow's. One precedes me bobbing its head,
hitching from one side to the other out into the grass
where each spear damply separate
strives for singularity from the clump.

*Sept. 29 - Oct. 3, 2004*


## A SEEMING PARALLEL

I wrote to a silence for those three years,
pruning my thoughts,
sending only sunshine.

The letters were read to you I was told;
you seemed to listen.
Perhaps you sensed the deception,
wrestled with the alien litany
of good things only.

Or, did you drift in and out of sentences,
following the cadence,
missing the text;
even as I these three long years
have merely traced the perimeter of existence,
unable to respond?

*Oct. 31 - Nov. 10, 1994*

## THE FINAL PHONE CALL

I could not understand what she said,
but it did not matter. Words are dead
when presence speaks.
Her substance came across the wires
into the receiver of my eyes.

*June 2, 2006; Aug. 27, 2007*

## NEGATING

"No! That's not what I said."
All of tomorrow crashed in my head
because you had
said what you said you hadn't.

Life slurried on in a stinging swelter,
the mind a baffle of why the lie,
the body a flutter of shut-down hopes:
I did not matter.

*March 20-21, 1999*

## GRACELESS

The seeds of madness are sprinkled
light as down on every head,
through every bone and sinew,
through muscle to the blood.

Soon we grow a little careless
and the days are drenched with shade.
The limits of possibility
crowd the familiar from its place.

There are no answers to the questions
short-circuited to the brain.
The whistling hint of madness
is a comforting refrain.

*June 30 - July 7, 1999*

## CIRCUMSPECTION

Before it all slips by,
I'll go again
because no sky
is bluer than yesterday's.

On each shore I've stepped
from East to West,
I've left no print that's evident
except for what my mind retains.

Memory can be a cruel thing,
turn an innocence to guilt,
resurrect an ancient pain
and let you suffer it again.

Without, how else to know
that you've been there,
that blue is bluer in retrospect,
and the beginning finds its end.

*Jan. 3 - April 2, 2004*


## THE OTHER WORLD

Yesterday a crow
touched down on my head.
Landing lopsided,
it tried again,
zooming in, scrunching
its feet against my scalp.

Uncertain of the nature of the threat,
I watched it loft
to the wire overhead
and meditate,
its feathers roused.

Seconds ticked by.
I flexed my jolted senses,
crisscrossed where beaks
and wings are king,
set a bag atop my head
and kept on walking.

*Feb. 19, 1997*

## LAST CHANCE

Autumn prods
the tardy blooms.
Slugs bloated
with morning dew
denude the fuchsia.
Not surprising that the earth
changes scent
from light to dark
chocolate,
nor that flesh shrivels
and bones wilt.
Winter requires
such preparation.

*Oct. 12-14, 2004*


## MY HOUSE

I am alone in this house
that has become the enemy
hiding what I set down,
sullying what I make clean,
impeding my movements,
jarring hands and knees.

"Get out," it clanks when I try to sleep.
The morning it allows the windows
is always a dirty gray, filmy with menace.

"You make me sick," it gargles.
"If you won't go, I'll fall apart around you."

*July 1-5, 2007*

## CURTAIN CALLS

Lashquick as dawn absorbed the night,
I caught the saucy pirouette
of Death the Harlequin.
He of multiple disguises
smirked and bowed and winked
himself into the bedpost.

Sometimes he melts before my eyes
fully discern his posturings.
He quickens breath and stops the heart
and puffs a dust into the throat.

His wily whisper at my ear
stirs shivers through my hair.
Then fingers needle-stitch my spine,
an alien ice burn.

Churlish clown,
I hang upon your turn of time,
the hiatus before oblivion.
When on the final night we meet,
what scene, what act am I to cue on?
What subtle guise will you adopt?

But what if you are human?

*Aug. 2 - Sept. 26, 1995*


## DRUNKS, FOOLS, AND CHILDREN

all may be found among these rocks
spat from the gravel mouth of the ocean.

Then comes me,
composite of all three,
moving unsteadily in the wash of waves,
turning my back to the incoming sea,
building houses out of sand.

*June 11-12, 2003*

## NOVEMBER POSTLUDE

The threat is there
but when it comes
it is only soft rain
in delicate parallels
so thin it barely
skims the skin.

*Nov. 19-26, 2012*

## DEFINITIONS

The crow, epitome of black,
has a silver sheen under morning sun.
Grass rain-turned varies its green.
The ditch retains the puddles' imprint
long after the memory of rain is gone.

However, how well-defined, nothing is forever.
Things lose their borders — forget, neglect,
perversely leak from their surroundings —
like inflated balloons tied to hold air
gradually wrinkle away to their beginnings.

The mind accepts what the senses send,
buckling under the weight of change —
the "is," the "was," the present, the past
jumbled together in uneasy peace.

*Feb. 17-21, 2010*

## APACE

is how it goes —
spring into summer
summer into fall
fall into winter —
residuals all.

*Dec. 28, 2008*

293

## SUMMATION

He asked if I lived alone.

> Funny, I thought.
> I live with all the people I have known,
> in all the places that I've been,
> with every dream I ever dreamed.

I don't.

*Jan. 22-23, 2012*

## LEARNING

The first time strips the face of innocence —
a bruise that burns, a stunning pain, a scar.
Through repetition insight disappears
and rote replaces what the senses felt.

Oh never seek to reach that height again,
to ache before and after wish expires.
What is the first will bear no replica.
Loss and gain are equal in the tomb.

*May 26 - June 1, 2003*

## EMBRACE THE BEAST

Without the beast that in abeyance lies,
no lyric form would ever grace the day —
no painting, sculpture, poem born of man.
Our world would be prosaic, shades of gray.

So we must laud the beast that hones our days
and sharpens well our appetite for pain.
Without his ministrations we'd be numbed
and posturing—the beast unknown, unborn.

## TALK TO ME

Have I silenced you, fear, –
burning  into the bones
halting the walk
dimming the sense
refuting the cry
of "All is well" –
by saying you are not the fear of death;
you are the fear of life?

*May 7-16, 2000*


## PRESCIENCE

I felt in my bones
the crease in the air.
My eyes turned craven:
No one was there.

Yet something moved vibrant
wherever I went.
The rooms stretched unending;
The presence?No doubt.

All day I kept turning
to see who was near
but substance eluded me –
I faced only air.

I knew in my bones
that much is unseen,
that wonder and hope join
to serve as a screen

for what's sensed yet unknown –
a half-conscious quest.
I anticipate vision,
revelation, insight.

*Dec. 7, 1999 - Jan. 3, 2000*

BANISHMENT

Well, hello, Yesterday.
You still here?
I told you we were all through.
Why do you persist,
offering that plate of leftovers?
I have had enough.

Today I'm accepting
a sweet October morning,
the blue absorbing the gray,
a thin suggestion of pink clouds,
and the undertone of bird chirps.
I have enough.

*Oct. 19-21, 2012*

INHALING THE UNIVERSE
(For Jake)

Gone to seed, each dandelion
is a microcosm, a constellation
prickling with its stabs of down,
lording it over the grass.

Years ago I carefully plucked one
and held it before my grandson,
showing by my pursed mouth
how to blow.
Instead he inhaled it
and, mouth frothing,
gave me a cloudy smile.

Wordless, I swabbed him out,
loosing the damp seeds to earth,
humbled by how much he had learned.

*Sept. 23-27, 2012*

## MIDSUMMER AFTERNOON

Summer's dreams are different,
sodden with heat, dizzying, surreal.

A small bird escapes a snapping dog,
slips out of its feathers
leaving them behind still shaped;
hops away,
its bones apparent through the naked skin.

You wake,
the sky intense, wired with electricity,
the afternoon stretched taut as a staked tent.

Time arrests,
a still-life painting pasted on the brain.
From the real bird world
a plaintive tremolo hums —
a burbling sorrow—
the mourning dove,
the mourning dove incessant.

*July 10-12, 2009*


## ARRESTED

It does not come back.
It won't.
It sits there,
a purple bruise
stiffened
in long-dead courage.

Who but a child
would want to pick apart
a frozen flower.

*Feb. 26-27, 2013*

## HARD TIME

"He came from nowhere,"
was all he said.
The scene shimmered crystal:
the broken child dead,
the crane a stilled monster,
the field bleeding red.

Every night since
he's lived it again—
the landscape, the face,
the thick globs of blood—
in a flattened dimension,
the cell of his brain.

*June 26-29, 2000*


## DISSIPATING

Fog,
knowing no impediment,
its time limited,
flows in quickly
obscuring details
until the world is
nothing but moist and swirl.

Fog,
spending its significance
in withdrawal,
melts invisibly
revealing color and form
until the world is
nothing but light and fresh.

> There are words
> but words do not capture
> the elusive —
> they only mimic its reality.

*April 1-3, 2011*

CURTAINS

The cruelty of August reigns
in subtle touches here and there.
Alyssum wilts, godetia fails,
and autumn taints the summer air.

I mark it well, the casual
duplicity of leaves and fern
that fade so slightly every day
they fool the eye to think it's June.

How many seasons have I worn
this barbarous indifference?
How little have I learned of change;
how much of its significance.

*Aug. 27 - Sept. 3, 2003*


LIFELINE

The lilies were ribbed-pink promises.
Days slid by, buds swelled without visible strain.
Slowly the petals broke free exposing the stamens
blood-red; by noon, dark wine.

In two weeks they mottled a dirty brown,
curled toward earth, the stamens rusted.

Now one by one the blossoms fall intact,
splayed ugly on the chunks of bark.
No trace of yesterday touches them
to hint at what they were.

*Aug. 31 - Sept. 1, 2011*

RESOLUTIONS

Memories plucked out
barely pock the skin,
but if deeper into the flesh
the healing takes longer;
into the marrow,
the residuals form scar tissue.

Age brings objectivity
and the unsought desire
to peruse these pluckings,
to feed to satiation,
knowing instinctively
there can be but the shadow
of understanding;
that confounding the senses
(those wild exhilarations)
is reserved only for the young.

*Dec. 18-30, 2007*


DOWN TO ESSENTIALS:
(A Couple of Loose Screws)

There are eyes
that strip off your flesh
so that, in memory, cold and wet,
you rattle down the night street,
a cacophony of bones,
white against black.

When the doctor said
sweeping his finger down the X-ray,
(a Rorschach print to you)
"That's really ugly,"
you had to smile.

You know what you carry —
your history of death
in bone and blood —
and that it differs little from anyone's
except for the eight-inch Blount plate
that has loosed two screws
and is your singular distinction.

*Dec. 8-11, 2003*

FRAMING

Night narrows down
to the rooms under the eyelids
where exploration begins
and memory dilutes the substance of the day.

Somewhere in dreaming lies the lie,
the real transposed to fantasy,
the shameful shaped until it's squared.

The sleeper can't be forced to see
the consequences of the past.
He changes them until he's freed
and tomorrow fills the emptied rooms.

*Feb. 24-29, 2004*


SEPARATION

Why do the shades of grief appear in tiers, in tiers?
Who wields the blade on the palette, selects the tiers?

Someone is scraping repeatedly on the canvas of my skull,
exploding, exploding the colors, multiplying tiers.

No mornings are predictable whether blue or gray or bleared.
This Oregon coast will brighten while dropping rain in tiers.

Either the undergrowth flourishes to fully sustain the new
or withers slowly unnoticed, disguised by tiers of tiers.

In brave blue spurts the lithodora colors the fragrant air
above its graying and rotting, tangled in murky tiers.

Midway through the summer, the scent of autumn stirs
with orange and russet promises, freshly hued tiers.

Candles are lit against darkness, spilling shadows to the floor.
One puff and they're extinguished, indiscernible tiers.

Countdown comes with dawn, the end of the beginning.
With you, Mary, the palette is blurry, blurred in tiers.

*Aug. 1-5, 2012*

## VALLEY WOMAN: PUZZLIN'

I think I'm livin' yesterday
'stead of today.
Reckon that ain't unnatchur'l
cause they's more days behind me
than is before.

Makes me wonder
if I'm jest summin' up
the pluses 'n minuses,
studyin' on why I went one way
'stead of the other
and if where I ended up
is where I'm s'posed to be.

*July 10-11, 2003*


## GONE

I shall construct my own little castle
out of secret happy words,
adding on rooms and turrets
until it is habitable only by me.
It will be centered in a maze,
drawing up short wayfarers
who stumble in seeking refuge.

Once when I was in college
a disgruntled art student sneered,
"You sit over there in your ivory tower."
Now I can revel in that fitting description.

*Dec. 20, 1997 - Jan. 7, 1998; Oct. 13, 2011*


## 2 PHAT

His waddle took the walk
but his smile overflowed it.

*June 19, 1996*

## MIRROR IMAGE

You haven't a window.
It's a mirror of one
that reflects the reflection
you've settled upon.

Thus what you see
is what you get.
The mirror breaks,
your vision forfeit.

*June 13-22, 2008*


## GROUPING

How simply they made an island
in the bustle of Burger King.
Sixteen of them at four tables,
one playing a guitar, another the ukelele;
the old woman singing in her native language,
clear as a mountain stream burbling over rocks.

We the outsiders munched our burgers,
remembering our families grouped.
Two together do not make an island when you're old.

*April 10-13, 1999*


## BROUGHT UP SHORT

A sudden lapse, a crumple of the bones —
a small unease displaces certainty.
The sixth of yesterday or fifty years aroused
disrupts the sequence that I know.
I am the robot in Cheops's tomb
who finds the door sealed off to one more room.

*Oct. 23- Nov. 3, 2002*

## VALLEY WOMAN: HUNKERIN' DOWN

I'm puttin' in my last licks 'round the yard,
gettin' us both ready
to hunker down for the winter;
shakin' out seeds inta my hand
'n scatterin' 'em in places
that look real lorn.

They's always spots
that never take to growin'
even though I cain't see no diff'rence
in the soil.

Anyways I'll scratch up the dirt a bit
and sprinkle these li'l black dots of seed
from the perennial pinks
–they'll grow most near anywhere –
'n maybe, come spring,
I'll get me an eyeful.

*Sept. 21, 1999*


## NO IMPRINT

He stripped it down
layer after layer
of old linoleum,
each with residuals:
a bobby pin
a flattened spider
two BB's
a rubber band
and a twist of twine –
not enough to reconstruct
the lives once lived
when that linoleum
was laid.

Late that night –
the new in place
pristine and shining,
a gloat of sense –
barefoot I padded
back and forth
establishing territorial rights.

Half-asleep
I saw no trace;
nothing marred
that gleaming surface.
It was as if I'd never been:
My prints had sunk
into the floor.

*June 23-25, 2000*


## OUTSIDE

I break off the thin dried stems of thrift
leaving them on the ground for the nest-builders
twittering domestically in this false spring of February.
The crocus is thrusting purple and yellow,
the azalea sprouting pink,
and I think of that old man reported missing,
his stark description
"a mind fighting a losing battle with time."

*Feb. 18-27, 2009*


## THE CHECK-OUT LINE

Was it enough?
His fingers bony and distorted
pinched a rain check.
A smile stretched his mouth.
Wrinkles had spent his face,
wrapped his cheeks to rounds.

Something old and careful left his eyes
and he giggled.
"I've got time, plenty of time.
You go ahead of me."

*Oct. 20, 1993*

## VALLEY WOMAN: RACIN'THE SUN

I bin chasin' my shadow since the sun come up.
Now here you be, lazyin' inta me,
givin' me two heads, four arms, four legs,
makin' me feel all fat and squatty
like I ain't done nothin'
but sit around stuffin' myself.

You jest take off now. I got work to do
else'n the sun'll ketch me at high noon
and flatten me right down
sose you can't tell me from my shadow.

*July 8-9, 1997*


## UNFINISHED

The only constant the soundless clock
with its precisely segmented ten-minute intervals:

"Are you in pain? You haven't released any medication."
 (Not enough of me here to make a decision).

The nurse presses the button anyway. I am a rag doll.
The night continues clashing its noiseless gears.

I am given ice in a cup.
I shift my arm for the blood pressure check,
admire a cloth doll the night nurse is making,
my timing and sentences seemingly adequate
but distant, alien, hollow;
unreal as a midnight bus- wait,
roadside in Montana, Route 1,
in the dead of winter.

*Nov. 5 - Dec. 25, 2005; Jan. 8, 2006*

# A COTERIE UNDER THE WILLOW

Three plastic flamingos cloister
under the dense willow,
exposed only when the wind swoops,
fanning out the branches.

All summer they chitter and clack,
bowered from dogs and cats
and passersby. In the slack
of late August, the talk dwindles.

Leaves are thinning; privacy,
less common. The wind, an intruder,
now becomes noisy,
drowning their voices.

They stand stark, faded
in their leafless room, alert
to the death of summer,
their silence sifting up the street.

A gray malevolence seeps,
permeates the clearing.
The quiet breathes a dire intent
of what they do when summer's spent.

They do not sleep, these weathered birds,
ominous in their rigid stance —stung
by a switch of season to plot, nefarious,
their gossip to disseminate in spring.

*Feb. 7, 2010; Jan. 27, 2013*

A CALIBRATION OF ALIENS

Is there anything foreign in your body?

"Yes," I said,"an eight-inch Blount plate
and a couple of loose screws."

Those aliens do their own smirking and winking:
I didn't need to,
but the memory gives me pleasure.

Just north of their position
three new immigrants have taken up residence,
drilled slantwise into the hip.

The wars begin again
with nothing in common except the host,
the bone which they inhabit.

I am a battleground for alien expression.
How in all that filthy stubble
can I tell my name?

*June 16-23, 1993*


LOST IN TRANSLATION

Dandelions age marvelously,
gray- capped like exploding rockets
the slightest stir of air can scoop
and disperse soundlessly.

Blooming clumps commune,
some twisting to get an audience,
others standing upright to impose
or lean in for a confidence.

But the silence is too loud to hear them.
Their language is yellow
translated voiceless in another dimension
where words do not matter.

*Oct. 15-18, 2008*

## VALLEY WOMAN : SHE SAID

Pain ain't got no color.
I'm tellin' you
it jest keeps pinchin'
but there's no black 'n blue
spots like you'd expect
to find where a hurt is,
like when you lose your sense
and trip on shadows.

It's sorta like a dust devil
jest suddenly there spinnin'
'n whirlin' 'round
without any reason
that you can see for it
or even guess.
It grabs a chunk o' you
but don't leave no trace.

*Nov. 2, 1993*

## GRADUATION

You never saw me.
I was always at the edge of your dream,
the unidentified,
the peripheral,
a shadow of nothing.

Not for me the embrace of the crowd—
hoping to be accepted
or spurning the possibility.
I couldn't play the game.

Now that I am free of longing,
with sag and shamble
absolving the blossom of my heart,
I can bask in the calm of being no one.

*Aug. 23-27, 2006*

ADMONITION

I long for a ghost of Christmas past.
For what have I to strengthen me
when memory fails to raise one tree
above another, one Eve, one gift,
one warming smile, one fat mince pie?

Then one pale specter rises saying
you have the moment only, same as ever,
and if you do not stop to savor
you will have no Christmas now.

*Dec. 26-30, 2012*


IN THE GARDEN

I have taken a hand in death,
dealing out poison pellets.
The slugs melt down in gelatin trails
quivering in the morning sun.

Quietly at their given moment
with no transfer of pain,
they stiffen in their thick brown sludge
and go to earth again.

Every survival warrants a death
to insure no dearth of blossoms.
But mourning blinds the eye to sense
and flowers are no recompense.

*July 19, 1995*


NARROWED

My world is as narrowed
as this stationery on which I write,
as this keyboard on which I type,
as this envelope into which I slide the obituary,
your history of achievements
with not a single word about you.

*May 26-28;  Oct. 19, 2002*

## NO WEASELING

How curious the sameness of each day.
No bungling clock has changed the month's marquee.
I would not have it any other way.

Familiar things have little to betray
their age —unlike the difference in me.
How curious the sameness of each day.

Sometimes the need to pause, to go astray,
is triggered by the calendar's decree.
I would not have it any other way.

For, I am older than these thoughts portray.
My words, my rhymes still echo futilely.
How curious the sameness of each day.

My dreams are tethered, held in trust —at bay,
the forfeits paid before I knew the fee.
I would not have it any other way.

Each little notch deflects what I would say
of how I measured out the century.
How curious the sameness of each day.
I would not have it any other way.

*July 30 - Aug.3, 2003*


## GOING OVER

I dance in  my dreams
full of wonder not grief
with dips and full swirls
to music half-heard,
one hand on your shoulder,
one hand in your hand,
I dance in my dreams
and I am so young.

*July 14 - Aug. 7, 2006; Sept. 2, 2007*

## DISAPPEARING DARK
(For Connie)

On the dark side the slugs feed,
gorging on leaves and fiber
but sliding away when the sun breaks through
into the flowered lithodora.

The rain with tentative fingers
plucks at the window glass.
Night swells out like a cape in the wind.
The dawn rides in on a star.

The fool in me whimpers—broken,
struck down by the advent of light.
Day blooms out of desecration.
The stone in my heart dissolves.

*May 1-3, 2000*


## ANDREW

He skirted the edges of charm,
tucked little French phrases into his speeches
(and they were always speeches),
never noticing that people bit the edges of their smiles
to keep from laughing.

At sixty-two inches, he was a giant.
After all, it was what was in the head
that made the man.
Now, wasn't it?

He strutted in his checked trousers,
stooping only to gather pine needles
clotted in the gutters of the street
so that he could claim a share in his wife's garden.

His was the soul of bigotry:
No one could measure up to him.
He never liked anyone except himself,
but he adored his wife.

*May 8-16, 2000; July 14, 2000*

## VALLEY WOMAN: SOMEONE TO DO FOR

Many's the time
I bin so shriveled up inside
I got no more feelin' for human'ty
than a rock.
Funny thing is
when I'm like that
I got no feelin' for m'self either.
It all comes down to
if you hain't got someone to do for,
you're just idlin'.

The way I see it
's like ivy crawlin' up a brick wall.
You gotta keep an eye on it
to know what it's up to
'fore it's done.
You hafta scrabble to keep those li'l bitty roots
from eatin' out the concrete.
Else some act o' nature like a big wind or a hard rain'll
cause the whole wall to fall in on itself.

Then it's all over
"n you got nothin' but leavin's
to start in on from the ground up,
tryin' to make sense outta all them pieces
soze you can fit 'em together again.

*Oct. 16-19, 1999*


## CLOSING THE BOOK

The well-known shadow in the wings —
the pent breath,
the very hover of when or now —
puts aside the scripted speech,
the monologue,
the dialogue,
the postures bred of imitation;
freely looses the borrowed trappings,
sweeps the curtain wide
with no remnant of disbelief
left clueless in the dark.

*April 30 - May 2, 2003*

INTIMATIONS

Here
is the remembered
breath of winter.
No dearth of scent,
a tickling of the nose,
a prickling of decay,
promises of compost.

Here
is the remembered
breath, not of death,
but of earth replenishing,
preparing for birth
in its own particular rhythm.

*Dec. 17-20, 2009; Oct. 19, 2011*


AFTER EASTER

In my private heaven
my lost son,
my dad and mom,
and thousands I knew
but left back East
and never learned of their demise
are shorn of pain
and wrong intention.
And on those glorious
unknown beaches
all my dogs run
free and ageless.

Here, God the Father
tenders heaven
even to me,
an earthly beggar.
When I take the cup
and eat the bread,
I know the warmth of being fed
the promise of salvation.

*April 14-15, 1998*

## SHEDDING TIME

Dead tree branches sprigged with moss
accumulate on the ground,
their dry whispers enticing.

The mourning doves' feathers snag,
puffy on the pine's green needles;
the crows' dark ones, like spent arrows,
barb the earth.

Spiders spin their final hammocks
in the autumn grass.
What you read in the quivering lace
is death, charmingly fashioned
for the unsuspecting.

Skin wilts.
The brain slips into the dormancy
of whimpering over what is that once was.

Going to earth,
our last communications
are strangely similar.

*Oct. 20-25, 2009*


## DECEMBER 30-31

The sky is falling rice-size
striking the roof and springing upward
in sprays like spirea.

It is fitting the year end in ice
melting off the calendar into history.

*Dec. 30-31, 2004*

## VALLEY WOMAN: SQUIRRELY

I been squirrely a-mornin's
gettin' myself accommodated to daylight.
Gotta ease up slow like a bucket out of a well,
all the time the weight tryin' to hold me down.

Night 'n me have jest got too friendly o'late.
Long 'bout one a.m. when the dark's sittin' heavy on my eyelids,
things start resurrectin'.

I'm eight, ten, maybe twelve years old
walkin' down Main Street ( it's the only one there is)
to my daddy's store,
remembrin' to run past the barber shop
sose that nasty Tyler won't have time
to whoop at me or make disgustin' suckin' noises.
I pass the ol' gentleman in the black suit
who always tips his hat to me (Mama says to smile at him),
go past the beer parlor holdin' my breath,
until there I am, the sun gone down behind the hills,
watchin' Daddy fastnin' up the awnings.

When I come to daytime, it's like I'm messin' round
in a space I don't know much about no more,
an ol' raggedy woman settin' her feet like flat irons
sose she won't fall over
an' lay there spinnin' round and round
no more'n a June bug on its back.

*Jan. 22-28, 1998*


## IN OPPOSITION

The fingers remember.
They play the chords, the trills
until the jealous brain asks,
"What's next?"

The hands suspend over the keys,
the fingers splayed, fluttering.
Baffled, they press down
at the brain's command —
discordant.

*March 17-19, 2012*

CRISSCROSSING

She has gone
past immediate response —
ganglia awry,
the brain misdirecting,
trembling to comprehend.

Someone will answer
while her heart disappears
against expectation.
Someone will cup the phone
against an ear,
interpret the sounds,
discover the need.

It is time.
The crows bring morning
with their raucous bark
routing the gulls a neighbor feeds —
the air heavy with the flutter
of wings,
protest,
giving over.

*Sept. 22 – Oct. 3, 2003*


DISTURB A SLEEPING FACE

When so much lies behind your face,
how is it possible to trace
enough to know the words
to take your measure?

And should I, by some blind sense
or capricious twist of chance,
stumble on  the recognized,
what poor tormented ghost will rouse
whispering words from yesterday,
wander on a dim-lit stage
to wrestle again with shadows?

*Nov. 4-13, 1996*

6:30 A.M.

Under a gentle sky
I am my mother's daughter,
sitting primly on the waiting bench,
hands crossed, ankles locked, mouth up-curved.

The morning stars have blinked out,
the wind still sleeps.
All the eternals glow serene and soft,
a blessing for the senses.

Waiting should be outside, like this,
where the finite blends into the infinite;
away from the closed doors,
shabby magazines, surgery-capped nurses,
the clanking of carts transporting supplies,
the flat-faced laboring clock.

I am my mother's daughter,
chin up, shoulders squared.
It is time to go, to go
past the vivid primrose,
the opening buds of crocus;
past all the planned perfection
and through the hissing door
to wait the final moments
with a clock that tells me lies.

*Jan. 27-31, 2010*


LOOKING BACKWARD

For fear
I stopped my lips from dissent,
smiled to appease,
accepted what was given,
and asked for nothing.

For love
I stopped,
smiled,
accepted,
and got what I asked for—
nothing.

*April 20-23, 2004*

# SOUNDING THE DEPTHS

I will use my time no more
peeling layers of melancholy
down to an edible core.

Nor will I feed on enmity,
exposing roots until they dry
to a fiber of duplicity.

I will do what I can't deny,
give service to a mocking tongue,
for the days grow smaller as I die.

Moment by moment I am wrung
dry as a bone bleached by the sun,
mute with the weight of songs unsung.

Is my claim to space so overrun,
I too halt in body, soul, and mind
to seek one last horizon?

*Oct. 17-22, 1995; Sept. 4-7, 2012*


# FORGETTING THE OASIS

Do not eat.
The body is tired of factory work
and longing to shudder
two hundred and eighty feet above a thin blue river.
That was the Pecos
a quarter of a century ago.

No shivers run now in recollection.
There is just a postcard, lifeless,
propped against a pencil folder
on my frowsy desk.

Memory lies loose
kicking up only a dusty sea
of tumbleweed, sage, sand,
and space emptying
from a gray road into the horizon.

*July 31 - Aug. 1, 1995*

## IN THIS WORLD A FAMILIAR

I dreamed a black dog
in a breach of the fence,
my daughter's Stanley
with his powder-puff muzzle,
waiting;
the cold in my heart
a vortex of losses,
hers and mine.

Last night he came
again — unbidden.
"No," I said,
"off the bed."

He roamed, hopeful
in his inimitable pattern,
powerful, determined,
his black fur gleaming.
A dream moment more
ended with a sudden pounce
of his four paws on the mattress.

I jarred awake,
my room an embrasure,
my room warmed.

*May 13-27, 2012*


## EVERYTHING TO ITS SEASON

October
douses its blazing moon,
rains on the dropped leaves,
shrinks the houses to their foundations,
and creeps out rattling its skeleton in the north wind
routing the spirits that reveled on its final day.

November
inhales the rank death smell, shuddering,
prickling our thinned blood,
tingling our fingers, icing our noses
until we recapture the evidence of life within us
in the soft white breath we expel.

*Oct. 31- Nov. 11, 2007*

## THE LEGACY

She kneels down, toe-deep in loam,
cupping the air in replica
of each bloom of tulip, iris, and alyssum;
pinching out dandelions and wayward viola.

The scent of pollen quickens
under her dirt-seamed hands.
Carefully sifting, she finds the fans
of the bleeding heart; thins
the encroaching tide of green
to let it crown the bed tomorrow
with plump lush reds —
this queen of hearts,
this touch of sorrow.

*March 28 - April 7, 1994*


## ASSUMING PRECEDENCE

Slowly as morning lengthens,
my shadow shortens,
crawling toward me
to cower at my feet.

Every noon I walk
in the dark of my own image,
sheltering its furtive quivering
as I move.

I am neither led
nor trailed
by this insubstantial
mimicking my movements
until, at high noon,
the diminishing moment,
it beckons me into the earth

*Sept. 22-24, 1997*

COMING TO TERMS

It is into the earth slow motion,
the bones feeling their prison of flesh
flattening, sagging in folds
over their contours.

It is down the rabbit hole
through the past, not in years
but in scraps hung askew
in unrelated space.

It is getting smaller,
looking through a keyhole
into rooms where you once lived
bright with impulse, spiced with motion.

It is the whisper of doors closing
just before you raise your eyes,
the flat stillness seeping into your mind
stirring the pages of yesterday.

It is the concentration of light and warmth
flowering a  riot in the skull,
the last high noon of heaven
before your shadow inhales you.

*Feb. 7-16, 1994*


THE HEART OF THE WOOD

Sudden as a blossom
the face you sought is there –
the spirit of the wood –
as if by touch
you gave it life
before your eyes could.

*Sept. 5-10, 2000*

## HANGOVER

Here is morning,
luminous, a huge pearl,
the shore pines crotched to hold it.

Nightmares recede
to their shadowy haunts.
There is nothing left to fear.

Except —
memory retains
the slam of running feet,
the darkness under the trees,
the tremble of the heart,
and always the amorphous entity,
the unknown pursuer.

*Oct. 9-11, 2009*


## ODD ONE OUT

For now,
your breath clouds glass
and dust makes you sneeze.
Day and night exchange places,
winter warms into spring,
sun and wind sear
and you harvest the difference.
Some things are
as they've always been,
but not you.

Tomorrow you'll wake
breathless
on some other shore,
your definition left behind
simmering like wet leaves in the gutter.

*Nov. 4-14, 2003*

## TURNING TO STONE

For months I watched my friend
turn to stone with ALS
and another
shuffle into rigidity
with Parkinson's.

Inside, my heart grew
old with recognition,
sustaining heights
greater than the depths
to which the body sinks.

From the beach
I selected agates
gargled smooth
over countless life spans.
I interred them
in jars on the windowsill.
They hold light.

*Oct. 11-13, 2002*

## SHADOWS

In that infinitesimal moment
just before the lights come up,
the theater dark and pulsing
with unexpelled breath,
you know it all,
the whole history of expectation.

The stage erupts in light
and the dream begins
with you timeless in your shadowy seat,
bone and blood and skin in mimicry,
a tenuous commitment to a non-existent world.

*July 13-17, 2005*

## STORMING THE FORTRESS

The great assault untamed is love.
A stammering, it feeds the pulse.
The reason shatters when it's gone.

Anticipation pricks the pores;
a spring unsprung awaits in vain
the great assault. Untamed is love

that struggles lest its absence shear.
The outcome is predictable:
The reason shatters. When it's gone,

the round is lost. Another sounds
to rise again, engage against
the great assault untamed. Is love

an isolate, the mind askew,
the boundaries so well-defined
the reason shatters when it's gone?

Insistent, nature leads us on:
Attempt again, once more to learn
the great assault untamed is love;
the reason shatters when it's gone.

*Feb. 6-9, 2001; Aug. 13-15, 2006*


## NON COMPOS MENTIS

I lifted my head to laugh at fear
and saw it had no face.
I squared my shoulders to face the day;
it disappeared in night.
I made a fist to punch out vengeance,
but you were no longer there.

There is light and there is dark
but I know only shades.

*Oct. 15, 1997*

## THE EYE OF THE BEHOLDER

The dropped flesh of the crimson tulip
bleeds under my heel on the concrete walk.
The first hot sun sears my winter arms.
Summer has begun the slow murder
of its predecessor —
the hydrangea sprawling over the daffodils,
the rose sharpening its spines on the anemones.

Giving over is never graceful.
Drying husks and browning fronds
wrinkle and totter,
retreat to their beginnings
in stringy rot.

I follow the flowering and demise,
greedily insatiable,
forever thirsty
for all things ephemeral,
knowing that autumn crowds summer
before winter shoulders in
stealing all  the color
from the bronze, the red, the gold.

*May 14-17, 1999*


## PRIME TIME

He was gone so long
that when he died
there was less of nothing.

Thus, here she goes round
the squaring of things,
the squaring of things.
Here she goes round,
here she goes round
at one o'clock in the morning.

And, here she goes round
the cobbler's bench.
She monkeys as the weasel,
cobbling puzzles every which way.
Pop! goes her reason.

*June 28 - July 2, 2012*

A COLOR BLIND
(To Laurie)

The artist said
there is red
in every living thing.

Red in the crow's feathers
under the sun,
red in the pine cone
the squirrel munches on,
red in the calla lily's
long white throat,
red in the tabby's
banded coat,
red in the fescue,
the banana slug,
red in the house fly,
the lightning bug.

A whisper of red
in each living creation —
but like the reddest of autumn
it may appear brown.

*April 23-26, 2002*


A LITTLE OF SOMETHING

Sometimes past evenings return
when you're tying your shoes
or spooning up the last of the stew.

Mama calls, "Come look at the sunset,"
and there it is over the river
where the old sycamore fronts the sky —
a pastel confection or a flaming fiesta.
You watch until it slides home behind the hill,
and the night drops like a cape ovor the valley.

The temporary will endure,
or what's a memory for.

*March 2; July 24, 2005*

## A HOUSE HAS A WOMAN'S NAME

The houses close down one by one,
shut their faces to the street.
The grass lengthens.
It is the time of purgatory
when all that was used, loved, cared for
distances itself from the owner
and is carried away.
What is there to
Luella's crystal-lit kitchen,
Faye's window of Martha Washington geraniums,
Myrtle's worn armchair disguised with fragile antimacassars?

The For Sale signs appear.
The houses like stamped images sit
in their fields of grass and dandelions.
Rhododendron and hydrangeas
bloom in their seasons.
But no Christmas comes
to these isolates of winter,
no shining lights, tinsel,
purfling of fragrant spruce.

Sound retreats.
The shadows shrink.
The doors are stiffening in their frames.
All that has passed is muffled.
I stutter down a street of names.

*Aug. 4 - Sept. 26, 1993*


## IN ABEYANCE

I walked on frosted grass this morning.
Hush, hush, it said.

Suspended,
a spider unreeled on a sun-gilt thread,
swayed in the current,
awaiting the loft to its destination,
that tethering point that gives its beginning an end.

*Jan. 15-18, 2009*

DECEMBER THIRTY-FIRST:
THROUGH THE HOURGLASS

They are streaming
through the winter woods
traceless on the chocolate-colored leaves
thick with rain—
years of shuttered scenes
loosened from the grip of memory :
tinsel and mangers;
turkeys and pumpkins;
fireworks and poppies;
crosses;
valentines and champagne.
Impossible to stay the flow.

They whip by—
unexamined,
screened too briefly—
until my eyes are only cupped rain
in the failed light.

The glass is empty,
the sand winked out,
the pyramid holding
only a fragile moment
before sifting down.

*Dec. 28, 1998-Jan. 4, 1999*


TWO-FACED

Raw morning scorches the throat.
The words come hard,
lie on the paper bruised.
Voiced, they drown
in the sodden air,
sticky mud,
northwind blasts,
bone-storming rain,
and create soggy islands
in a sea of earth.
In all this gray of nothing
one dandelion blooms.

*Jan. 8-22, 2008*

DYING BACK

Who will buy these dahlias
days past their prime,
the price dropped
from four ninety-eight
to ninety-nine?

Who will note the lovely
in the  faded colors,
wrinkled petals,
drooping heads?

The old woman sees
the pot is dry,
neglect has hastened the demise.
The leaves are promising;
the stems, sturdy.
The perennial dies to live again.

She will buy.

*Sept. 13-15, 2003*


THE OTHER ROOM

Children are in the other room.
Giggles like bubbles pop up and erupt.
Whispers of secrets stir in the air,
hang tardy in the limpid night.

Sometimes it is grandchildren;
sometimes, my own;
or my sister and I
pillowing our voices,
exploding with snorts.

I stand at the door,
swallowing the urge
to re-enter childhood
never fully left;
to soften the longing,
blur my insight
that I too hang tardy
in the limpid night.

*July 9, 2000; April 2, 2005; Aug. 7-8, 2010*

RIGHT OF PASSAGE

Some doors are not open to you
even though you think
you can turn the knob,
step over the threshold
and arrive welcomed.
Close to the surface,
not deep down,
you know once in
that you will sense a rat.

Years ago in Mexico
you found one swimming in the toilet.
Your husband took one look,
tripped the flush and dropped the lid.
No one used that room again.

Some doors are better left shut.

Forget dare or risk
or puerile interest.
Open the wrong one?
Either you or the rat will scurry.

*Sept. 30 - Oct. 1-5, 2008*

THE ICTUS

It's going to gaff you and it does —
suddenly piercing and hooking you
right out of your cozy dream of creek and river
there by the sycamore, its dead branches
fingers against the long summer sunsets.

Once you are scooped up, netted,
you writhe hungry, leaving dormant
those settings out of this world but from it,
aware that however gradually you retrieve them
you cannot resurrect the rhythm.

*Sept. 16-20, 2009*

*ictus: metrical or rhythmical stress or beat in utterance;
the stress that falls on syllables in poetic rhythm*

## THE DRIFT OF AUTUMN

The slow moon,
clouds of the palest coral
doubling and redoubling
rolling out a carpet for the sun —
Dawn.

*Oct. 31 - Nov. 16, 1999*

## ALL THERE IS

I think he became his father slowly,
a mender of shoes
behind the grimed store-front window.

When I walked past,
memory told me who he was
or had been.

How many years had he sat there,
tapping and gluing and sewing,
the town dying around him
until the shop was just
a place to go to six days a week?
Or had he left, found the world too big,
and come back
to let his youth dissipate
into leather and rubber and polish
and old men's talk?

It was only a moment,
long enough to glance in,
but his eyes bruised me
with their apathy.
I still wear the scar.

*Feb. 8-12, 1999*

## VALLEY WOMAN: SUFFRIN' FOOLS

Sot in his ways he is,
the ol' fool.
Trouble is he got hung up in his twenties
'n never left 'em.

I seen 'im smackin' his lips
over the young girls
'n gittin' right up 'gainst 'em
like as how they might be int'rested
in what he got to offer.

Us ol' women we know better.
Once our looks done faded into the wallpaper
we don't go makin' up to a man
'cause we know
he'd never even
give us the time o' day.

They ain't a single one o' us
thet'd wanna be young ag'in,
least of all try to make out like we wuz.

*Dec. 7-9, 1998*

## CLOSURE

She put up a fence
with a bold "No Trespassing" sign.
She couldn't be bothered.

It grayed along with her
as the children,
blocked from a shortcut to school,
graduated to cars.

No one noticed when
despite fence and sign
the ultimate trespasser moved in
and had his way with her.

*April 23-25, 2003*

## MID-NOVEMBER

This patch of earth that I call mine,
softened with autumn rain,
has offered me a springtime bloom
before the winter comes.

Beside the leafless pink smoke tree
a daylily splays its petals,
a shock of April yellow
among the dead and dying.

I could wish for more I know,
but wishes are not in season.
Far greater is this gift of life,
a shout of affirmation.

*Nov. 8-17, 2003*


## TO BE OR NOT
(For Jeannette)

That two-year old dark-haired girl
spurned my teasing sing-song
"I see you in the window."

"That's not me; that's my reflection,"
she responded, eyes flat in reprimand.

She has grown and I have aged,
both changed in each other's eyes,
but from this disintegration,
this slipping, sliding-down descent,
I know her truth by the mirror
and want to howl it out,
"That's not ME!
"That's my reflection."

*Jan. 6-9, 2010*

WOOLGATHERING

No past can be recalled for memory lies.
The shards collected are mere compromise.

What was sought – the light— an exercise,
a false enlightenment hard won
from a drift of scent
a taste of salt
a broken smile
and eyes that darkened with a trace of pain.

The truth exacts a penance in reprise.

*Jan. 14-23, 2011*


LAPSE

I have fallen out of time
into the brash field of dandelions,
my eyes burnt yellow,
so filled with light
I've forgotten how to move –
senseless as a scarecrow
pinned in the drowsy air.

*July 26-28, 2000*


JULY DAY

This is the time to disappear
after the lightning and thunder,
today— so fair,
so unexpectedly bright
with the blue hydrangeas
supplanting the scent of roses
I cannot feel the earth
beneath my feet.

*July 20-22, 2012*

335

## VALLEY WOMAN: JOURNEYIN'

I knew soon as I woke up
it was an ol' woman's mornin'
with last night's warm still hangin' 'round.
When yer young, that's garanteed
so you never notice; yer primed up
for what's comin' next.

Mostly now I'm comparin'
what wuz to what is.
I'm sorta like a bird
comin' back to its ol' nest,
scootin' 'round inside it
sose it'll fit jest right.
Gets me thinkin' my whole life
was prep'ration for comin' home.

*Nov. 30 - Dec. 4, 2012*

## PORTRAIT: MIDDLE-AGED DREAMER
(Somebody's Ex)

He has his own epiphany
he shapes into a world,
sunlight flowing between his hands
loosing globular rainbows
luminous in his sight.

An innocent —
he plants no seed,
he tills no soil,
he knows no reveille or taps.

His world is shaped ephemeral
forever in his mind.

*May 27 - June 2, 1999*

## THE CADAVER'S BONES

Hey there, Lady,
you got my bones.
Just so you don't forget,
I cinch them up sometimes.
That crackling sound you hear?
Comes from me laughing
when you wince and groan.

I want you to know
a cadaver has no choice
of where his bones go.
Maybe you'll find out some day;
that is, if you got anything
worth salvaging when you kick off.
But, being so old, you'd probably
just come back at night —
float around the house
of whoever got them,
scaring the pants off him —
wailing,
"I
want
my
bo-o-nes
back."

*Oct. 6-8, 2009*


## SUMMER MORNING

I opened the window.
The sky flew in,
an arpeggio of birdsong
of fog and of blue.

I whispered hello
to this mélange all new,
and slipped past my losses
when the sun broke through.

*June 18 - July 5, 2012*

## VALLEY WOMAN: STOLEN PROMISES

The dark's bin comin' in
slow and careful
like a knife through frozen butter.
the same way those deer come in
and chewed up the red zinnia seedlin's,
chomped the shoots off the glads,
and stomped over my dahlias.

I had to remind myself
that they only took what I was promised
and it weren't no savage loss
if I looked at it jest right:
What was goin' to feed me later
don't make no never mind
to a critter that's hungry now.

*June 29 - July 21, 1998*


## THE LETTER BOX

I wrote you my life,
highs and lows,
the fearful and the beautiful.
It is all there in that box,
twenty-five years of letters,
one-third of a lifetime.

I shall place them in order,
read the words of that woman
and seek a relation to this one.
But not yet.

Not now so soon after you've left;
not before I try the new identity,
no one's daughter,
and the alien sound of it washes away.

*Aug. 6, 1998*

## SECOND SIGHT

The thin skin between awake and asleep
harbors the feast for the senses.
The silent show materializes —
the principals, the scenery, the bit players
assuming their importance —
all unchanged from what memory selected.

Odd these replays, these excursions
into memories buried fifty years.
Odder still that those pregnant moments
no longer spark the blood,
that one can read clearly, cleanly, logically
what was really taking place.

*March 13-15, 2009*


## VALLEY WOMAN: STARTIN' OFF RIGHT

When I wanta
piece of mornin'
that don't start out gray
'n seemin' hopeless,
I look out the winda
at thet bunch o' or'nge glads
a-tiltin' to the South
the way the north wind blew 'em.

Then I get my trow'l
'n go slug-huntin',
hove them greasy li'l critters inta the street.

I figure I done my share
to presarve what's pretty and helpless
from those pesky petes
there ain't no way
to fight back aginst.

*Aug. 19, 1998*

TIMELESS

The sea anemone quivers
with the water's flow;
its land counterpart shivers
at the wind's touch –
each accepting its constant
while we persist in
our chilling journeys,
withering in our efforts to live
with both present and past.

*April 29 - May 2, 2010*


THE PENULTIMATE YEAR

The morning mist is slower to disperse,
each shrub and tree and flower overblown,
mid-summer's fruit just not so sweet in taste,
the tick of time too audible to miss.

*July 6-10, 2004*


VALLEY WOMAN: 50/50

I gotta nuff o' today
without havin' to deal with
what yesterday's throwin' up.
Too much lost
'n nothin' to be done 'bout none of it.
Seems like I jest fergot my 'bility
to say I'll think 'bout it tomorra.
I ain't no Scarlet O'Hara.
I keep remembrin' that my daddy
always said he didn't believe in hell
'cause you got all the hell you're ever gonna git
right here on earth.
The best I can do is to say
if this is hell today,
jest wait 'til tomorra.

*Oct. 9-12, 2004*

## SIMPLE JUSTICE

I am my own Medusa
confronting a likeness of stone
daily in yesterday's mirror.

Blistered under the nemesis of old sins,
I mind my hours frugally,
growing distance between past and present,
the freight shunting in my brain.

Only the shards of ecstasy
crackle in these dry bones,
bladed thin as shadows,
blanched with ancient pain.

Yet, when the morning opens,
the nebulae dispersed,
I shall not be wakened.
My pulse did not keep time.

*June 12-23, 1994*


## THE INVITATION

C'mon, seduce me.
Forget the times I've spurned you,
laughed at your efforts,
seen through your wiliness,
peeled away your disguises.

Never mind
that I'm no vision of pulchritude.
We're all alike in the dark.

You must be wonderfully circumspect
with your years of practice,
but — leave the scythe outside.

*May 25-29, 2011*

## AFTER THE FACT

The woman waits.
The air she breathes is small;
it feels like dust.
The only substantial,
the parquet floor under her feet.

Silence hangs in the closet,
lays its alien sheen on the door,
intrudes into the maze her mind is.

The woman waits:
no release from time
jerking by the second
over the face of her watch,
no promise of a different tomorrow.

*Sept. 30 - Oct. 8, 2006*


## POST-ANESTHESIA

Half corpse, you're wheeled
parallel to heaven, two floors from earth,
lifted to a bed, attached to bottles
by needles and threads of tubing.

The brain blown struggles
through knots of scattered wits,
patching patches —
a seamed identity that will not share
the stint in hell when your corpse lay there.

Nothing foreign, nothing known,
the afternoon severed by a missing hour.
Silence shouts from the anteroom of hell:
Your body profaned! Your mind a tomb!

*Aug. 30 – Sept. 2, 1993*

## VALLEY WOMAN: NOTHIN' O' VALUE
(For Scott)

They never had nothin',
none of them Jenners,
but they clung like leeches
wherever they got a hold.

Sose it was no surprise
to me nor to my brother
when we found Red's shelter
smack dab in the middle
of the second island.

Now half the valley is a river
and there's two big islands in it
gettin' eaten out as you can plainly  see
by the grass dangling its roots in the water.

Well, right in there Ol' Red had took his woman,
settin' up housekeepin' under an ol' tarpaulin,
choppin' down some of the white pines
where my brother had started an arboretum.
(My brother owns this island
and he was still young enough to be plantin' dreams).
Real pretty it used to be in that sunny clearing
with the criss-cross shadows of the pines
layin' on the ground.
Now all there was was Ol' Red's garbage,
a knife, a broken-handled axe, and sludge,
the kind you wouldn't want to think about.
It was like a big scab oozin'..

My brother tore down the tarp, folded it,
and stuffed it and the knife in the canoe.
Paddlin' home we met Red and his woman
comin' back in an ol' squared-off rowboat.
He spoke to my brother, sheepish-like,
maybe suspectin' we had the salvage from his place,
maybe knowin' he had no rights layin' out a home
just because nobody was around
But he'd been there, left his mark.

Like I told you,
they was all leeches,
but when you pulled 'em off
a part of 'em always stuck to you.

*July 3-6, 1994*

## A POEM WITHOUT MISERY

I just want a little taste
from the banquets of yesterday,
enough to tease my senses,
to punctuate the hours,
to diminish the pallor of hope
for what can never be,
to know the hunger of a flower
for the enticements of the bee.

*July 27, 2003*




## THE WAITING ROOM

The room is there to enclose you
with all the dreads harbored for years.
They ease around your hunched shoulders,
slither down your arms,
chill your torso,
and creep into your shoes.

So, you walk up and down the halls
resurrecting your past,
away from the laboring clock
and the rank stench of measured time.

The room waits whether you do or not.
It staked its claim eons ago in your name.

*Jan. 12-15, 2005*

## BETWEEN THE TICK AND THE TOCK

The cap and bells ring in the new
in barbaric year-end custom;
but on the last split chime of midnight
the silence is louder yet.

I am impaled, caught on that pivot,
tight with unused breath.
My bones feel stark, my flesh like starch:
I'm all alone forever.

Kiss off the old, kiss in the new.
Sound the horn and pop the bottle.
Wish everyone the best of years.
Shake, rattle, and roll.

I cannot play the integrant,
I cannot kiss my spouse,
I cannot numb the outgrown year
and turn myself about.

Each year I hope my island
joins the mainland, forgets the sea.
Each year I hope to be attuned
that that bell may sound for me.

*Nov. 1966; Sept. 2011*

## REVELATION

It's all right to disappear.
I learned in church this morning
that Saul became Paul.

*March 22, 2013*

## AFTERMATH

"I don't want to make it any harder for you," he said.
So he left without a goodbye.

True, it was no harder,
yet prickly pockets of air
pass up and down the empty hall,
the curious substance that isn't there
but marked our whole existence.

*Apr. 14-28, 2013*

## ADDENDUM

All is clear
but what I seek—
the elusive clue
to fifty years of silence.

*March 22, 2013*

# BEFORE THE TRICK OF SILENCE

Before the trick of silence,
hurl me a paltry part:
one lightning smash of ecstasy
to shock the lions enskulled.

Pink me out of pattern.
Shred me to an aster spear
that I may be a straw of gold
to prick the end of summer.

Swath me with riotous sunsets.
Spring my brain with freezing hail.
Pour me a jug of thunder
to shoulder up my griefs.

Carve me to a fine-bone point
before I blaze down to dust.
Baffle me with nudity:
strip my senses' skin.

I shall hover hourly on the quiver,
scratch the rime of impending frost,
flay the scalps of old disguises
before Death finger-prints my eyes.

*Dec. 1965*

## A NOTE ON THE AUTHOR

Mary Mansour Durel grew up in a small coal-mining town in West Virginia, the second of seven children. After being graduated from West Virginia University with a B.A. in English and an M.A. in Education, she taught school in West Virginia, Maryland, Ohio, Illinois, and Washington State.

She, her husband, and their children lived for several years in Washington, California, Mexico, Georgia, and Oregon. For twenty years she performed in community theater. At present she lives in Bandon, Oregon.

She may be contacted at mmdurelpoetry@gmail.com

Made in the USA
Charleston, SC
09 July 2013